MW01012232

UN OFF- END ABLE

BRANT HANSEN

WITH SAM O'NEAL

HOW JUST **ONE CHANGE** CAN MAKE ALL OF LIFE BETTER

Harper*Christian* Resources

CONTENTS

A NOTE FROM BRANT

We are now living in an "anger incubator."

That phrase is from a psychology professor at the University of California at Irvine, and I think he's right on.[1] I imagine you agree, too. Our culture is fraught with anger. It's everywhere, and no one seems to know what to do about it.

In Christian circles, we're often taught that anger can be a very good thing and that we're supposed to use our "righteous anger" to make things better. But here's a question: *Is that really what the Bible says about our anger?*

And what are we really supposed to do about it? Are Christians supposed to be as angry as everyone else? Are we supposed to be angry about all the things in the world that we think displease God? Is our anger *actually* righteous? How do we know? And how long are we supposed to hold on to our anger?

Or . . . is there another way?

Yes, we live in an angry world that lacks answers and seems to spin on an axis of offense. But what if followers of Jesus were known as the most unoffendable people on the planet?

Can we—and *should* we—become unoffendable as followers of Christ?

Brant Hansen

HOW TO *USE* THIS *GUIDE*

If you look up *offended* in a dictionary, most entries will say something about feelings of anger and resentment. For example, the *Cambridge Dictionary* defines *offended* as being "upset or angry, often because someone has been rude." There is even a helpful illustration provided: "Many staff members were deeply offended by his email."[2]

It's the *taking* of offense, and the presumption we are entitled to be angry at another person, that we will be tackling in this study. Over the course of the next six sessions, you will discover what the Bible says about ideas such as "righteous anger," what rights followers of Christ have to be offended, and what it means to really forgive another person. In the process, you will discover not only that you *can* choose to be unoffendable . . . but that you *should* choose to be unoffendable. All the time. Every time.

Now, before you begin, keep in mind that there are a few ways you can go through this material. You can experience this study with others in a group (such as a Bible study, Sunday school class, or any other small-group gathering), or you may choose to go through the content on your own. Either way, know that the videos for each session are available for you to view at any time by following the instructions provided on the inside cover of this study guide.

Group Study

Each of the sessions in this study are divided into two parts: (1) a group study section, and (2) a personal study section. The group study section provides a basic framework on how to open your time together, get the most out of the video content, and discuss the key ideas together that were presented in the teaching. Each session includes the following:

- **Welcome:** A short note about the topic of the session for you to read on your own before you meet as a group.
- **Connect:** A few icebreaker questions to get you and your group members thinking about the topic and interacting with each other.

- **Watch:** An outline of the key points covered in each video teaching to help you follow along, stay engaged, and take notes.
- **Discuss:** Questions to help your group reflect on the teaching material presented and apply it to your lives. In each session, you will be given four suggested questions and four additional questions to use as time allows.
- **Respond:** A short personal exercise to help reinforce the key ideas.
- **Pray:** A place for you to record prayer requests and praises for the week.

If you are doing this study in a group, make sure you have your own copy of the study guide so you can write down your thoughts, responses, and reflections—and so you have access to the videos via streaming. You may also want a copy of the *Unoffendable* book, as reading it alongside the curriculum will provide you with deeper insights. (See the notes at the beginning of each group session and personal study section on which chapters of the book you should read before the next group session.)

Finally, keep these points in mind:

- **Facilitation:** If you are doing this study in a group, you will want to appoint someone to serve as a facilitator. This person will be responsible for starting the video and keeping track of time during discussions and activities. If *you* have been chosen for this role, there are some resources in the back of this guide that can help you lead your group through the study.

- **Faithfulness:** Your group is a place where tremendous growth can happen as you reflect on the Bible, ask questions, and learn what God is doing in other people's lives. For this reason, be fully committed and attend each session so you can build trust and rapport with the other members.

- **Friendship:** The goal of any small group is to serve as a place where people can share, learn about God, and build friendships. So seek to make your group a "safe place." Be honest about your thoughts and feelings, but also listen carefully to everyone else's thoughts, feelings, and opinions. Keep anything personal that your group members share in confidence so that you can create a community where people can heal, be challenged, and grow spiritually.

If you are going through this study on your own, read the opening Welcome section and reflect on the questions in the Connect section. Watch the video and use the prompts provided to take notes. Finally, personalize the questions and exercises in the

Discuss and Respond sections. Close by recording any requests you want to pray about during the week.

Personal Study

The personal study is for you to work through on your own during the week. Each exercise is designed to help you explore the key ideas you uncovered during your group time and delve into passages of Scripture that will help you apply those principles to your life. Go at your own pace, doing a little each day—or tackle the material all at once. Remember to spend a few moments in silence to listen to whatever God might be saying to you.

Here is a general outline of each week's study:

- **Day 1:** You will refamiliarize yourself with the content presented during your group time and start to consider how it may apply to your life.
- **Day 2:** You will read a passage on a key topic covered in the group time and underline and highlight key words and phrases that stand out. You will also engage in a few questions and exercises designed to help you apply the truths of that passage from Scripture to your situation.
- **Day 3:** You will read a key passage on another key topic that was discussed during your group time and start to break down some practical ways that you can apply what it says to your life.
- **Day 4:** You will be encouraged to reach out to another member of your group so you can both process a bit of what you've learned this week. You will also be provided with a few questions and exercises to go through together.
- **Day 5:** You will be given time to reflect and respond to everything covered during the week and read the chapters in the book for the next session.

Note that if you are doing this study as part of a group, and you are unable to finish (or even start) these personal studies for the week, you should still attend the group time. Be assured that you are still wanted and welcome even if you don't have your "homework" done. The group studies and personal studies are intended to help you hear what God wants you to hear and how to apply what he is saying to your life.

So . . . as you go through this study, be listening for him to speak to you as you learn about what it means to be *unoffendable*.

Schedule

BEFORE GROUP MEETING	Read chapters 1–4 in *Unoffendable* Read the Welcome section (page 3)
GROUP MEETING	Discuss the Connect questions Watch the video teaching for session 1 Discuss the questions that follow as a group Do the closing exercise and pray (pages 3–11)
PERSONAL STUDY – DAY 1	Complete the daily study (pages 14–17)
PERSONAL STUDY – DAY 2	Complete the daily study (pages 18–20)
PERSONAL STUDY – DAY 3	Complete the daily study (pages 21–23)
PERSONAL STUDY – DAY 4	Complete the daily study (pages 24–26)
PERSONAL STUDY – DAY 5 (before week 2 group meeting)	Read chapters 5–8 in *Unoffendable* Complete any unfinished personal studies (page 27)

THE MYTH OF RIGH- TEOUS ANGER

Everyone should be quick to listen, slow to speak and slow to become angry, because human anger does not produce the righteousness that God desires.

JAMES 1:19-20

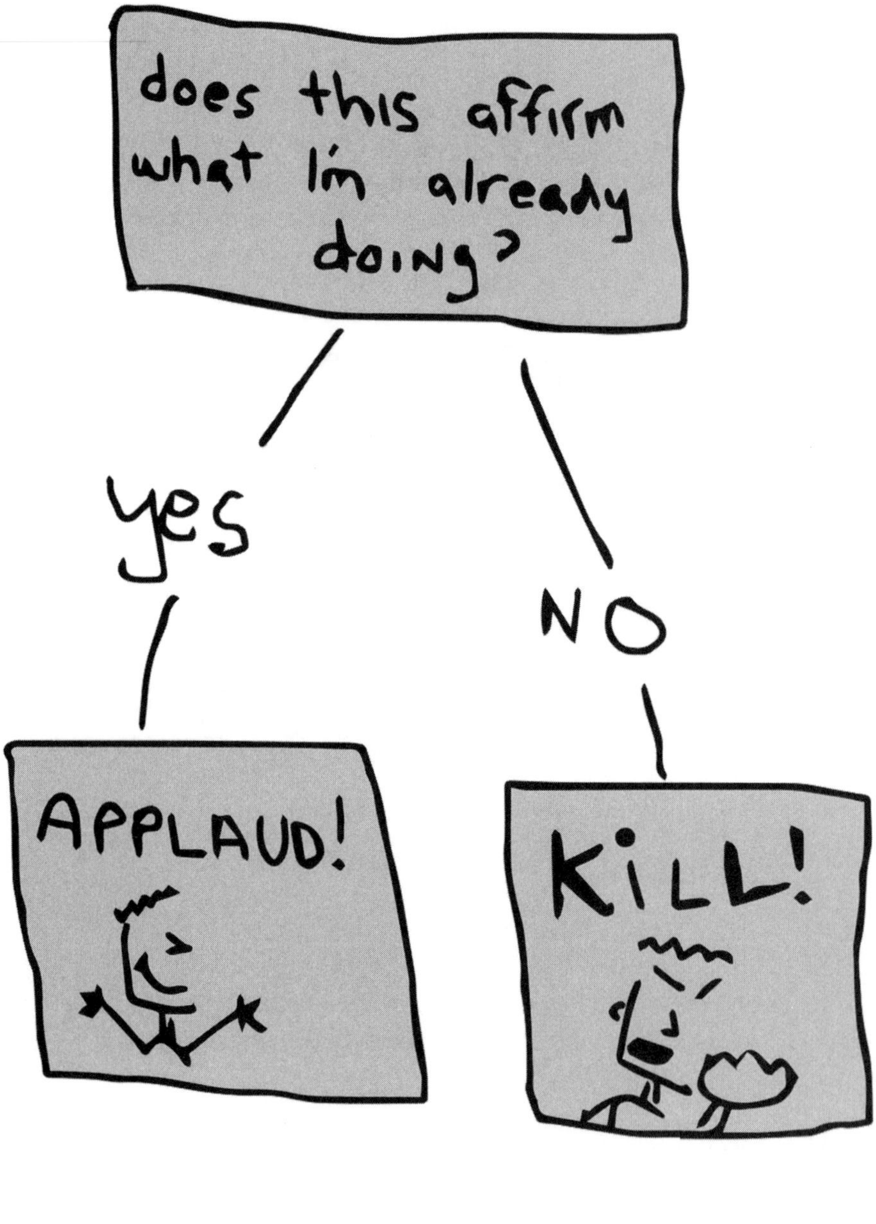
does this affirm what I'm already doing?
yes
NO
APPLAUD!
KILL!

WELCOME | READ ON YOUR OWN

People think I'm crazy when I talk about this topic . . .

. . . until they don't. (I hope.)

Most of us have grown up with a certain idea about "good anger" (or "righteous anger") and "bad anger" ("unrighteous anger"). But I'm going to challenge what we think we know.

Re-thinking (literally, what repenting means), is difficult for me. I get stuck in my own ideas very easily. But this is how we grow. I'm convinced God has things to show us, and if we're open to them, it'll require a lifetime of re-thinking that leads us to better ways of living.

So, if this topic today is particularly challenging for you—and what I'm saying is certainly counter-intuitive to the ways of our culture—thanks for giving it a shot.

CONNECT | 15 MINUTES

If you or any of your group members don't know each other, take a few minutes to introduce yourselves. Then, to get things started, discuss one of the following questions:

- How would you describe your primary goal or hope for participating in this study? (In other words, why are you here?)

  — or —

- On a scale of 1 (rarely) to 10 (regularly), how often do you experience the emotion of anger in a significant way? Explain your response.

WATCH | 20 MINUTES

Now it's time to watch the video for this session, which you can access by playing the DVD or through streaming (see the instructions provided on the inside front cover). As you watch, use the following outline to record any thoughts or concepts that stand out to you.

I. The main idea of this study is counterintuitive, and it might even seem a little crazy at first. But here it is—*we can choose to be unoffendable.*

    A. There is a way that we normally process ideas (see the illustration on page 2.) We want to be affirmed . . . and if we're not, we get angry!

    B. As Christians, we've been taught that anger is sometimes awesome and sometimes terrible. We've been taught that there is *righteous* anger and *non-righteous* anger.

    C. We believe that we are *supposed* to get offended at times because there is righteous anger. And we are to *stay* angry because we are supposed to stand up for what is right.

II. The reality is that while the Bible has a lot to say about anger, very little of it is positive—especially when it comes to *human* anger.

    A. A verse that people often memorize to justify their anger is Ephesians 4:26: "When you are angry, do not sin" (NCV). Anger is not a sin . . . so therefore we should get angry.

B. But this is not the whole verse. The second half of Ephesians 4:26 tells us to "be sure to stop being angry by the end of the day" (NCV). We're supposed to get rid of it.

C. The Bible is very consistent on this point. But unfortunately, what we often do is try to justify our anger and conflate it with God's anger.

III. The reality is that there is no such thing as righteous anger in the Bible for humans. It doesn't exist.

A. There *is* such a thing as righteous anger in the Bible—it just belongs to God. He is entitled to vengeance because he can be trusted with it. Instead, we are supposed to do something very different, radical, and countercultural. We are supposed to *forgive* other people.

B. In James 1:20, we read that our anger can't be used in the service of producing God's righteousness. The world needs us to take action, not to get angry.

C. Our anger doesn't do anybody any good. In fact, it only clouds our judgment. What the world needs are people who actually do things motivated not by anger but by love.

IV. The work of a follower of Jesus is to serve as an instrument of forgiveness in the world.

A. Jesus told a story about an unmerciful servant to demonstrate how important forgiveness is in our lives. We have been forgiven of a great debt, just like the servant. For us to then turn around and *not* forgive others is counter to how the kingdom of God works.

B. Jesus is giving us an easier life. Yes, forgiveness is hard, but it's way better than living our entire lives thinking we're supposed to be angry at everybody for what they've done.

C. We can actually say at the beginning of the day, "I'm going to forgive people. Stuff is going to happen, but this is what it means to follow Jesus, and I'm going to do it."

DISCUSS | 35 MINUTES

Take some time to discuss what you just watched by answering the following questions. There are some suggested questions below to help you begin your discussion, but feel free to use any of the additional questions as well as time allows.

SUGGESTED QUESTIONS

1. Our foundational beliefs and opinions about anger are often formed in our younger years, especially in light of our families. We learn what anger is and how to process it by observing those closest to us. What were you taught about anger as a child?

2. The phenomenon of "righteous anger" is not only prevalent in the church but also in our culture. There is a sense that sometimes we are correct to be angry or even that we are *supposed* to be angry. How has your life been shaped by this idea of righteous anger?

3. Forgiveness is the antidote to anger. It's what helps us let go of anger. Thinking back to your past, when have you experienced the power of forgiveness in a meaningful way?

4. Another key to successfully letting go of anger in your life is to recognize (and re-member) just how good, gracious, and merciful God has been with you. What are some of the biggest ways you have been influenced by God's goodness and grace?

ADDITIONAL QUESTIONS

5. Think about some of the specific ways our culture offers its opinions about anger—through movies, TV shows, books, news headlines, celebrity headlines, and so on. How would you summarize the message our culture is teaching about anger?

6. Now do the same exercise for forgiveness. What are the most consistent messages our culture communicates when it comes to the value and practice of forgiveness?

7. What is the point of Jesus' story that he told to his disciples about the unmerciful servant? What does the story reveal about the way God expects us to treat one another?

8. Let's say you decided right now to forgive someone—to let go of your "right" to be angry at that person and instead to offer the same forgiveness to him or her that you have received from God. What would that process look like?

RESPOND | 10 MINUTES

As mentioned in the video, Christians sometimes use Paul's words in Ephesians 4:26, "When you are angry, do not sin" (NCV), as divine permission to hold on to their anger. So, as you close out your time this week, take a look at that verse in its broader context to see what Paul was *actually* saying about anger. Do this on your own and then share as a group as time allows.

> [25] Therefore each of you must put off falsehood and speak truthfully to your neighbor, for we are all members of one body. [26] "In your anger do not sin": Do not let the sun go down while you are still angry, [27] and do not give the devil a foothold. [28] Anyone who has been stealing must steal no longer, but must work, doing something useful with their own hands, that they may have something to share with those in need.
>
> [29] Do not let any unwholesome talk come out of your mouths, but only what is helpful for building others up according to their needs, that it may benefit those who listen. [30] And do not grieve the Holy Spirit of God, with whom you were sealed for the day of redemption. [31] Get rid of all bitterness, rage and anger, brawling and slander, along with every form of malice. [32] Be kind and compassionate to one another, forgiving each other, just as in Christ God forgave you.
>
> Ephesians 4:25–32

What is the main message that these words from Paul communicate about anger?

When have you been able to "get rid" of something harmful in your life?

What commands are contained in this passage that followers of Jesus should obey?

PRAY | 10 MINUTES

Praying for one another is one of the most important things you can do as a community. So use this time wisely and make it more than just a "closing prayer" to end your group experience. Be intentional about sharing your prayers, reviewing how God is answering your prayers, and actually praying for each other as a group. When you do come to a close, express your desire to obey God on these subjects of anger and forgiveness. Ask him to speak with your group over the next several sessions and reveal his will for any anger that is present in your lives—and what to do with it. Use the space below to write down any requests mentioned so that you and your group members can continue to pray about them in the week ahead.

Name	Request

Personal STUDY

Anger isn't always easy to talk about. For one thing, like most emotions, it is highly personal. For another thing, it can be a big source of pain in your life. This is especially true if you've been on the receiving end of angry words or actions from other people. It's also true if you've struggled to keep your own anger under control.

The point is this: it's not always easy to talk about a subject such as anger in front of other people, even when you know and trust them. There are some subjects we all naturally keep private. Close to the vest. This is why this guide includes both a *group* study section and a *personal* study section. As you've already seen, it can be helpful to hear other people share their insights and experiences on a topic like anger. But it can be just as helpful to process those ideas in your own space, in your own time, and at your own speed.

So let's get started on that processing right now. The next few pages feature four days of personal study (plus a day to catch up on your reading) to help you think about your own experiences with anger and forgiveness. In this first week, you will work with the material in chapters 1–4 in *Unoffendable*. On the final day, you will also have time to catch up on any exercise that you were not able to complete during the week and also read chapters 5–8 in preparation for the next meeting.

SCAVENGER 📷 HUNT

Now, even though you will be studying on your own during the week, you should still be interacting with your fellow group members. A great way to do this is to set up a group text that includes every member. In addition to checking in with each other on prayer requests and what you are learning, you can also do a weekly scavenger hunt! Here's how it works. Each week, you will be given an object to find based on a key prop featured in the video. Your task is to locate that object (or something that represents it) during the week, take a picture of it, and send it to the other members on your group chat. The only rule is that it has to be an object in real life—not a picture you found online or in a magazine. We will start off with an easy one . . . a baseball bat. Bonus points for the group member who finds the most beat-up looking one!

Day 1

EMOTIONAL HINDSIGHT

The phrase "hindsight is 20/20" has great application when it comes to our emotional states. It can be hard to think rationally about strong emotions in the present. We rarely have the ability to step back and say, "Wow, I'm feeling really sad right now." Or, "Hey, I am grumpy today, so I should figure that out before I hop onto this morning's call."

This emotional blindspot applies to most of our strong feelings: happiness, fear, sadness, confusion, bitterness—and anger. How many times have you heard yourself say, angrily, "No! I'm not angry!" Thankfully, our emotional vision gets clearer when we've got some distance. We can recognize our feelings better from the past than the present. So, that is what you are going to do for today's personal study: use that emotional hindsight to get a better understanding of how you are impacted by anger.

1. Think back to the last time you remember feeling genuinely angry. A moment when you saw *red*—when your blood boiled. Sit in that moment and chew on it with your mind and heart. As part of this process, use the space below to draw a picture that represents the cause of your anger. (If drawing a picture sounds silly to you, just go with it. The goal is to help you zero in on the *cause* of your anger in a way that goes beyond your mind—to get your eyes and fingers involved. Don't worry about your drawing skill. No one needs to see this but you.)

2. When you look back on that moment, what made you feel so mad? (Be honest with yourself. Be honest *for* yourself. Honesty is the first step on the road to growth.)

How did your anger affect you? How did it affect others around you?

If you could change one thing about that experience, what would it be? Why?

3. What emotions are you feeling right now as you contemplate that moment from your past? Write down everything that comes to mind.

4. Read the excerpt below from chapter 2 of *Unoffendable*, and then answer the questions that follow.

> In the Bible's "wisdom literature," anger is always—not sometimes, *always*—associated with foolishness, not wisdom. The writer recognized that, yes, anger may visit us, but when it finds a residence, it's "in the lap of fools" (Ecclesiastes 7:9).

> Let that sink in. When anger lives, that's where it lives: in the lap of a fool.
>
> Thinking we're *entitled* to keep anger in our laps—whether toward the sin of a political figure, a news network, your dumb neighbor, your lying spouse, your deceased father, whomever is perfectly natural, and perfectly foolish.
>
> Make no mistake. Foolishness destroys.[3]

When have you seen or experienced this connection between anger and foolishness?

Foolishness is often portrayed as silly or harmless in today's world—think Homer Simpson or the latest comedy from Hollywood. But where have you seen evidence to support the claim that foolishness is ultimately destructive?

5. Read the excerpt below from chapter 3 of *Unoffendable*, and then answer the questions that follow.

> Forgive in the big things and the small things. Don't take offense.
>
> In fact, the stuff that usually might offend us is a huge opportunity! Jesus told us we will be forgiven as we forgive others.
>
> Fact is, most of us just don't get *that* many opportunities to forgive. Once I realized that, traffic went from being an exercise in anger to "forgiveness practice." Life is so much better that way.

I used to be scandalized by others' moral behavior. I'm just not anymore. It frees up a lot of mental space, and we probably need more of that, to pause and reflect on what matters in life. Sure, I've used my free mental space for baseball statistics and Duran Duran lyrics, but I can do better. So can you.[4]

Where do you have opportunities right now to practice forgiveness?

When has forgiveness helped to make your life better?

6. Think back to that recent moment when you got angry—the one you drew a picture about on the previous page. What might have changed in that situation if you were focused on forgiveness rather than anger?

Day 2

SLOW TO ANGER

You have to love the book of James in the New Testament. Bible books are kind of like kids in that we're not supposed to have favorites, but you have to appreciate the no-nonsense, take-no-prisoners, accept-no-excuses approach that James takes in his letter. The wisdom he relates speaks to us at the core of who we are. So, let's take a moment to see what James had to say on this subject of human anger. Read the following passage three times:

> [19] My dear brothers and sisters, take note of this: Everyone should be quick to listen, slow to speak and slow to become angry, [20] because human anger does not produce the righteousness that God desires. [21] Therefore, get rid of all moral filth and the evil that is so prevalent and humbly accept the word planted in you, which can save you.
>
> [22] Do not merely listen to the word, and so deceive yourselves. Do what it says. [23] Anyone who listens to the word but does not do what it says is like someone who looks at his face in a mirror [24] and, after looking at himself, goes away and immediately forgets what he looks like. [25] But whoever looks intently into the perfect law that gives freedom, and continues in it—not forgetting what they have heard, but doing it—they will be blessed in what they do.
>
> James 1:19–25

1. What ten observations strike you about these verses?

1.	2.
3.	4.

5.	6.
7.	8.
9.	10.

2. Which of the verses above have a direct application to the topic of anger? Underline the verses that apply. How do these verses contribute to your understanding of what anger is?

3. How do these verses contribute to your understanding of why anger is harmful?

4. In this week's group time, you talked about the need to not just get angry about something but actually take action. What does James say about taking action?

5. Use the following scale to rate your "anger speed." In most situations, how quickly do you get angry when you are confronted by something you don't like?

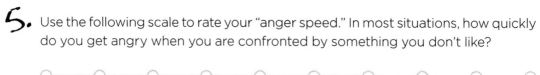

| 1 | 2 | 3 | 4 | 5 | 6 | 7 | 8 | 9 | 10 |

[Very slowly]   [Very quickly]

6. Look again at verse 25, where James talks about "freedom." What are some ways that anger can rob us of freedom?

Day 3

THE ANTIDOTE TO ANGER

In this week's group time, you saw that forgiveness is the antidote to anger. Forgiveness is what allows us to let go of our anger rather than keep clutching it to our chests like some cursed talisman. Forgiveness is important, and we're going to talk about what it means to forgive and how to forgive throughout this study. But first, we are going to focus on the words of Jesus. Actually, we are going to focus on a *story* from Jesus. Here goes:

[21] Then Peter came to Jesus and asked, "Lord, how many times shall I forgive my brother or sister who sins against me? Up to seven times?"

[22] Jesus answered, "I tell you, not seven times, but seventy-seven times.

[23] "Therefore, the kingdom of heaven is like a king who wanted to settle accounts with his servants. [24] As he began the settlement, a man who owed him ten thousand bags of gold was brought to him. [25] Since he was not able to pay, the master ordered that he and his wife and his children and all that he had be sold to repay the debt.

[26] "At this the servant fell on his knees before him. 'Be patient with me,' he begged, 'and I will pay back everything.' [27] The servant's master took pity on him, canceled the debt and let him go.

[28] "But when that servant went out, he found one of his fellow servants who owed him a hundred silver coins. He grabbed him and began to choke him. 'Pay back what you owe me!' he demanded.

[29] "His fellow servant fell to his knees and begged him, 'Be patient with me, and I will pay it back.'

[30] "But he refused. Instead, he went off and had the man thrown into prison until he could pay the debt. [31] When the other servants saw what had happened, they were outraged and went and told their master everything that had happened.

[32] "Then the master called the servant in. 'You wicked servant,' he said, 'I canceled all that debt of yours because you begged me to. [33] Shouldn't you have had mercy on

21

your fellow servant just as I had on you?' ³⁴ In anger his master handed him over to the jailers to be tortured, until he should pay back all he owed.

³⁵ "This is how my heavenly Father will treat each of you unless you forgive your brother or sister from your heart."

Matthew 18:21–35

1. Take a moment to unpack this story. Go back through the verses above and circle every word or phrase that connects with a human emotion. Write those in the space below.

2. Look at verse 21. What prompted Jesus to tell this story to his disciples?

3. Who are the main characters in the story? What actions do they take?

4. Write down verse 35. What did Jesus mean when he said *"this"*?

5. Use the "bricks" below to write down some obstacles you can think of that prevent people from being able to offer forgiveness to others.

6. Which of the obstacles listed above make it especially difficult for you to obey Jesus' command from verse 35 to "forgive from your heart"?

Day 4

REFRAMING ANGER

On Day 1, you reviewed a moment of anger from your recent past. Today, you are going to reframe how you might handle that anger in the future based on this idea of being unoffendable—of choosing to forgive rather than hold on to your grievances.

1. Use the space below to imagine a scenario for tomorrow in which you encounter a similar circumstance to the one that made you feel angry in the past. Flesh out that scenario by describing the scene, drawing a picture, making a list, or whatever method you prefer.

2. Now use the following questions to unpack the way you would like to respond if you were to face such a situation tomorrow. How will you recognize the fact that you're feeling angry? What thoughts or sensations can clue you in to the reality of your anger?

3. What would you like to say in that moment? Spend some time thinking of the right words, and then write them down.

4. What would you like to do in that moment to resolve the situation? Be specific.

5. Based on what you've encountered so far in this study, write down three action steps you can take this week to begin making your life better by letting go of anger. Again, be specific and realistic. "Don't get angry" is not a likely solution. Instead, a more realistic action step might be, "Recognize when I am feeling the emotion of anger." Now it's your turn:

Action step 1:

Action step 2:

Action step 3:

6. Now for the hard part! (Maybe.) Contact someone from your group and talk through your answers to each of the above questions. (Call, meet for coffee, engage in a long and meaningful text conversation, or whatever method of communication works for you.) Share with that person how you would like to respond the next time you have an opportunity to get angry, and then listen as that person shares with you. Write down your reflections and takeaways below after you have that conversation.

Day 5

CATCH UP AND READ AHEAD

Use this time to go back and complete any of the study and reflection questions from previous days this week that you weren't able to finish. Make a note below of any revelations you've had and reflect on any growth or personal insights you've gained.

Spend the next two days reading chapters 5–8 of *Unoffendable*. Use the space below to make note of anything in the chapters that stands out to you or encourages you.

Schedule

WEEK 2

BEFORE GROUP MEETING	Read chapters 5–8 in *Unoffendable* Read the Welcome section (page 31)
GROUP MEETING	Discuss the Connect questions Watch the video teaching for session 2 Discuss the questions that follow as a group Do the closing exercise and pray (pages 31–39)
PERSONAL STUDY – DAY 1	Complete the daily study (pages 42–46)
PERSONAL STUDY – DAY 2	Complete the daily study (pages 47–49)
PERSONAL STUDY – DAY 3	Complete the daily study (pages 50–51)
PERSONAL STUDY – DAY 4	Complete the daily study (pages 52–54)
PERSONAL STUDY – DAY 5 (before week 3 group meeting)	Read chapters 9–12 in *Unoffendable* Complete any unfinished personal studies (page 55)

WHAT HUMANS ARE LIKE

Because of the miraculous signs Jesus did in Jerusalem at the Passover celebration, many began to trust in him. But Jesus didn't trust them, because he knew all about people. No one needed to tell him about human nature, for he knew what was in each person's heart.

JOHN 2:23-25, NLT

WELCOME | READ ON YOUR OWN

Here's something that's astonishing to me: God knows me better than I know myself and still wants to be with me.

I don't even really want to be with me. Not for long, anyway. Honestly, I get tired of my own inner voice. I get aggravated with the breathtaking immaturity and self-centeredness in my own head.

But God knows me better than I do. He knows my real motives, and somehow he isn't scandalized. Yes, I'm messed up, but he's somehow not shocked by me. He doesn't walk away. If I turn to him, he comes running.

Like I said, that's astonishing.

This session is all about being more like him when it comes to how we react to other messed-up people.

CONNECT | 15 MINUTES

If you or any of your group members don't know each other, take a few minutes to introduce yourselves. Then choose one of the following questions to discuss as a group:

- What is a key insight or takeaway from last week's personal study that you would like to share with the group?

  — or —

- In a typical week, how often do you feel shocked or scandalized by the behavior of other people? Explain your response.

WATCH | 20 MINUTES

Now it's time to watch the video for this session (remember that you can access this video via streaming by following the instructions printed on the inside front cover).

As you watch, use the following outline to record any thoughts or concepts that stand out to you.

I. Understanding who humans actually are—who we have been since the very beginning—is core to living an unoffendable life and practicing radical forgiveness.

  A. We have to quit being in constant shock when people do things or say things that we do not approve of. This is just the way humans are . . . deep in their hearts.

  B. Jesus understood the human heart. In one place in Scripture, it actually says that no one had to tell him what humans are like, because he knew their thoughts (see John 2:25).

  C. This is not intended to be a guilt trip but just an acknowledgment of reality so that we can stop being shocked at what people say and do.

II. Once we acknowledge that people are messed up, we can start to make friends with them, because we understand that they are going to be broken.

    A. When we adopt this point of view, people will actually want to hang around with us, because we will be the least judgmental people they know.

    B. The apostle Paul wrote that we are not a good judge of other people's intentions because we can't even judge our own motives (see 1 Corinthians 4:1–4).

    C. When we choose not to be offended by others—to not be scandalized by their behavior—it leads to us hanging in with them for the long haul.

III. Jesus is giving us a better and lighter way to live when it comes to dealing with others.

    A. Forgiveness is genius, radical, and excruciating. It requires us to deny ourselves and choose not to hold our anger against other people.

B. We choose to forgive others because it is not about what they did to us but what God did for us.

IV. Repentance is key to living this life of radical forgiveness—being able to admit when we're wrong.

A. There is a proverb that says the first to testify always seems right until he is cross-examined. The first to testify in our own heads is *us*.

B. Jesus constantly tells us to humble ourselves so we can entertain the thought that we just might be wrong about something.

C. We can go into the day knowing that people are going to do all the messed-up things that they are capable of doing. We can practice forgiving them when they do.

DISCUSS | 35 MINUTES

Take some time to discuss what you just watched by answering the following questions. There are some suggested questions below to help you begin your discussion, but feel free to use any of the additional questions as well as time allows.

SUGGESTED QUESTIONS

1. Words like *Christian* and *Evangelical* mean different things to different people. Some of those associations are positive, while some are negative. In your experience, what are some things our culture believes to be true about followers of Jesus?

2. Judging someone or being judgmental is looked down upon in today's culture. But judging others and being judgmental is also something all of us do pretty much every day. In your mind, what does it mean to judge another person?

3. In this week's teaching, you were given several examples of Christians who were compelling in their communities because they chose to not be shocked by others—to be unoffendable. Who in your life has made following Jesus seem positive and attractional? Why?

4. Self-righteousness, or the inability to admit when you're wrong, is a common element in religious people and religious behavior. How have you been burned by self-righteousness in your experiences with others? In your own life?

ADDITIONAL QUESTIONS

5. Human sinfulness should be an undisputed reality in our world because the evidence is plastered seemingly everywhere we look—the news, social medial, gossip around the water cooler. Where have you seen evidence recently that confirms people are messed up?

6. Now consider that same question for yourself. When have you been confronted recently with the reality that you are messed up—that you have issues that need to be dealt with?

7. How easy or difficult is it for you to admit that you are wrong about something? When is a time that you can recall in your life when clinging on to the idea of being "right" cost you in a relationship?

8. Humility is a key ingredient to being unoffendable. How would you define humility in your own words? What is it and what does it look like in your day-to-day life?

RESPOND | 10 MINUTES

In this week's teaching, we mentioned that the Bible says Jesus "did not need any testimony about mankind, for he knew what was in each person" (John 2:25). In other words, Jesus was very aware of the foibles and failures surrounding human nature. Below you will find another passage that illustrates Jesus' understanding of our drives and motivations as human beings. Have a volunteer read these verses out loud and then discuss the questions that follow.

> [25] When they found him on the other side of the lake, they asked him, "Rabbi, when did you get here?"
>
> [26] Jesus answered, "Very truly I tell you, you are looking for me, not because you saw the signs I performed but because you ate the loaves and had your fill. [27] Do not work for food that spoils, but for food that endures to eternal life, which the Son of Man will give you. For on him God the Father has placed his seal of approval."
>
> [28] Then they asked him, "What must we do to do the works God requires?"
>
> [29] Jesus answered, "The work of God is this: to believe in the one he has sent."
>
> [30] So they asked him, "What sign then will you give that we may see it and believe you? What will you do? [31] Our ancestors ate the manna in the wilderness; as it is written: 'He gave them bread from heaven to eat.'"
>
> [32] Jesus said to them, "Very truly I tell you, it is not Moses who has given you the bread from heaven, but it is my Father who gives you the true bread from heaven. [33] For the bread of God is the bread that comes down from heaven and gives life to the world."
>
> [34] "Sir," they said, "always give us this bread."

> [35] Then Jesus declared, "I am the bread of life. Whoever comes to me will never go hungry, and whoever believes in me will never be thirsty. [36] But as I told you, you have seen me and still you do not believe. [37] All those the Father gives me will come to me, and whoever comes to me I will never drive away. [38] For I have come down from heaven not to do my will but to do the will of him who sent me. [39] And this is the will of him who sent me, that I shall lose none of all those he has given me, but raise them up at the last day. [40] For my Father's will is that everyone who looks to the Son and believes in him shall have eternal life, and I will raise them up at the last day."
>
> [41] At this the Jews there began to grumble about him because he said, "I am the bread that came down from heaven." [42] They said, "Is this not Jesus, the son of Joseph, whose father and mother we know? How can he now say, 'I came down from heaven'?"
>
> John 6:25–42

What motivations were driving these people and their interactions with Jesus?

Based on the above passage, what can we learn about Jesus' priorities and values? What does he want for his followers?

Recognizing our own brokenness is one of the key steps we can take toward becoming unoffendable. What actions can you take this week to jumpstart that process?

PRAY | 10 MINUTES

Bring your gathering to a close by talking with God together as a group. Be courageous in confessing your own brokenness and your desire to judge others based on their brokenness. Ask God to present your group with opportunities to embrace humility and radical forgiveness in the coming week. Use the space below to write down any requests mentioned so that you and your group members can continue to pray about them in the week ahead.

Name   Request

_____   _____
_____   _____
_____   _____
_____   _____
_____   _____
_____   _____
_____   _____
_____   _____
_____   _____
_____   _____
_____   _____
_____   _____
_____   _____
_____   _____
_____   _____
_____   _____
_____   _____
_____   _____
_____   _____
_____   _____

In the first session, we focused on the destructive nature of anger in our lives and on the false belief that "righteous anger" is a good and necessary part of living as a Christian. We also introduced forgiveness as a kind of antidote to anger—a way we can set ourselves free.

In this session, we pivoted to highlight one of the key causes of anger in our lives. Namely, the people we encounter every day in our culture—and really, our entire culture itself—are broken, which means those people say things and do things that we find unacceptable. They act in ways that shock us or make us feel scandalized, and then we respond with anger and judgment. The end result of all this is a vicious cycle. Broken people make other people angry, which leads to judgment and offense, which leads to more brokenness, which leads to more anger—and on and on it goes.

Thankfully, we can break free from this cycle by taking a couple important steps. First, we can be honest with ourselves about our own failures and our own brokenness—we can be realistic about the state of our own human hearts. Second, we can embrace humility instead of judgment, understanding that we, too, are broken. In this week's personal study, we will explore both of these themes. Before you begin, if you are reading *Unoffendable* alongside this study, you might want to take a few moments to review chapters 5–8 in the book.

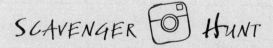

The backdrop for this week's video was a jury box. Keeping with this theme, your task is to find a court-related item—such as a gavel or a barrister's wig—and send it to your group. Remember that credit is awarded for finding something that represents these items if you don't happen to have these objects lying around. (Hint: a hammer or a white wig will work). Extra points for the group member who actually wears the wig!

Day 1

MAKING IT PERSONAL

So far, we have thrown around a lot of general terms and pronouns in our exploration of what human beings are like. *People* are broken. *They* are messed up. *Everyone* needs to address the reality of their mistakes and failures.

It's easier when we use such pronouns. After all, it's not a problem to talk about sinfulness and struggles when we keep everything at arm's length. But it doesn't really help us, either. It doesn't move anything forward. So let's get personal. In today's study material, you are encouraged to examine "what _____ is like," with the _____ being *you*. This is a chance to take a realistic look inside your mind and heart and be honest about your own brokenness.

1. Think back to the last time you truly felt disappointed with yourself. This doesn't mean last Tuesday when you forgot to take the garbage can out to the curb. We're talking about the last time you said or did something that made you feel frustrated with yourself. Remember, honesty leads to growth! Use the space below to record that moment in a way most comfortable for you—draw a picture, tell a story, make a list, or write a quick journal entry.

2. What emotions did you experience as you completed this exercise? Write down all that came to mind.

If you could change one thing about that experience, what would it be? Why?

3. Read the excerpt below from chapter 5 of *Unoffendable*, and then answer the questions that follow.

> I'm not shocked anymore. I want to be like Jesus: "No one needed to tell him what mankind is really like" (John 2:25 NLT).
>
> So humans are judgmental? Okay. Established. There are self-righteous people who self-describe as Christians, and there are self-righteous people who self-describe as atheists. They're self-righteous about different things, sure, but it's a very human thing to the core.
>
> That caustic email? I had to let it go. People are messed up. I know this because I talk to millions of them, and I'm messed up. This should not be daily news: *"I can't believe how crazy these people are . . ."* I've had to adjust my expectations and stop being offended.
>
> Look, you have free will, and you can be perpetually shocked and offended. But be honest: Isn't it kind of exhausting?
>
> This is not cynicism; this is living with realistic expectations—the very same understanding of our nature that Jesus has.[5]

The dictionary definition of self-righteousness is "confident of one's own righteousness, especially when smugly moralistic and intolerant of the opinions and behavior of others."[6] In what areas of life are you smug or intolerant about the opinions or behavior of others?

What are some topics that regularly cause you to feel shocked? Scandalized? Angry? Explain your response.

4. Think for a moment about this question from the quote above: "Look, you have free will, and you can be perpetually shocked and offended. But be honest: Isn't it kind of exhausting?" How would you answer that question right now?

What are the biggest sources of emotional stress in your life right now? Make a list.

What items could you remove from that list (and from your own shoulders) if you become unoffendable?

5. Read the excerpt below from chapter 7 of *Unoffendable*, and then answer the questions that follow.

> Jesus said that if we come to him, he'll give us rest (see Matthew 11:28). I'm discovering how multifaceted that is. As a kid, when I heard he'd said that, I had no idea what he was talking about. Looking around at all the church people, it seemed to me that Jesus had sure given them a lot of stuff to do.
>
> But as a young man, after I'd had some theological training and some time to really reflect on this . . . I still didn't understand it. Honestly, I thought maybe it meant after we're dead. *Then* we'll finally get some rest. Jesus will give us a break after a life of doing stuff. He'll help us rest in peace, or something like that.
>
> Now I understand that Jesus was talking to a weary, religion-soaked people. They'd been given so much to do and so many rules to follow. So many rabbis had expounded so much the right ways to do things, and Jesus was saying, "My way is easy to understand. Kids understand it. It's you adults and 'experts' who like to make things complex. My teachings are simple at heart."
>
> I love that so much. He's offering sweet relief from religious burdens. But he's doing even more than that. When we pay attention to what he's actually saying, like in the Sermon on the Mount, and actually put his principles into practice, we find life to be more restful.
>
> Still, it's up to us. My kids are older now, but I want them to know that. They're free. God knows what's best for us. He offers peace. He offers rest. But he lets us choose.[7]

When was the last time you experienced a season of rest? What were you doing? What made it so restful?

What are some religious expectations or self-righteous habits that are blocking you from experiencing that kind of rest in your spiritual life? What burdens might you be placing on yourself or others that are keeping you from the rest that Jesus offers?

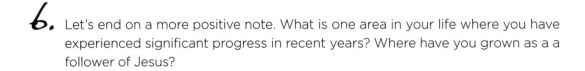 Let's end on a more positive note. What is one area in your life where you have experienced significant progress in recent years? Where have you grown as a a follower of Jesus?

Day 2

THE PROBLEM OF HYPOCRISY

When we think about people who are religious and self-righteous, one term that comes to mind is *Pharisee*. The Pharisees were members of the religious system in Jesus' day. They were supposed to teach, exhort, and encourage the people based on what God had revealed through his Word. Instead, they drifted into the all-too-familiar pattern of elevating themselves at the expense of those whom they were called to serve.

In the Bible, we find that whenever Jesus confronted the Pharisees, he did not specifically confront their sinfulness. *Everyone* with whom Jesus interacted with was sinful—his disciples, his friends, the people he healed, and the like. Instead, we find Jesus criticizing the Pharisees for their *hypocrisy*—for assuming they were righteous and everyone else was sinful and needed to be taught a lesson. Here is one example from Scripture. Read the following passage out loud and answer the questions that follow.

> [23] "Woe to you, teachers of the law and Pharisees, you hypocrites! You give a tenth of your spices—mint, dill and cumin. But you have neglected the more important matters of the law—justice, mercy and faithfulness. You should have practiced the latter, without neglecting the former. [24] You blind guides! You strain out a gnat but swallow a camel.
>
> [25] "Woe to you, teachers of the law and Pharisees, you hypocrites! You clean the outside of the cup and dish, but inside they are full of greed and self-indulgence. [26] Blind Pharisee! First clean the inside of the cup and dish, and then the outside also will be clean.
>
> [27] "Woe to you, teachers of the law and Pharisees, you hypocrites! You are like whitewashed tombs, which look beautiful on the outside but on the inside are full of the bones of the dead and everything unclean. [28] In the same way, on the outside you appear to people as righteous but on the inside you are full of hypocrisy and wickedness.
>
> Matthew 23:23–28

1. Circle all of the images or illustrations that Jesus used in these verses to describe the Pharisees. What do those images communicate?

2. What actions or attitudes does Jesus condemn in these verses?

3. How would you define *hypocrisy*? What is it and what does it look like in someone's life?

4. Jesus said of the Pharisees, "You strain out a gnat but swallow a camel" (verse 24). What are some "gnats" that religious people get worked up about in today's world? What are some "camels" they often ignore?

5. Christians often exert peer pressure on other Christians to behave "correctly." What are some ways that you have seen those in the church push people to clean "the outside of the cup and dish" rather than focusing on what is inside?

6. In Matthew 23, we read that Jesus mourned for the Pharisees. He said, "Jerusalem, Jerusalem, you who kill the prophets and stone those sent to you, how often I have longed to gather your children together, as a hen gathers her chicks under her wings, and you were not willing" (verse 37). Where are you currently resisting Jesus' call to freedom from hypocrisy? Where are you resisting his call to be free from being offended?

Day 3

MOTIVES OF THE HEART

In yesterday's study, we saw that Jesus pronounced several "woes" against the Pharisees because of their hypocrisy. But it's important to point out that not *all* the Pharisees were hypocrites. Some rejected their religiosity in order to become leaders in the early church.

Consider the apostle Paul, who described himself as a "Hebrew of Hebrews" (Philippians 3:5). He was hyper-religious during his early years—and probably hyper-hypocritical as well. But everything changed when Paul encountered the risen Christ. He let go of his religious obsession with the law and earning salvation and focused instead on God's grace.

Because of this new focus, Paul found freedom from the need to judge others and freedom from caring about what others said when they judged him. I mentioned this passage in the video teaching for this session, but take a moment to read it over a few times, and then work through the questions that follow.

> ¹ This, then, is how you ought to regard us: as servants of Christ and as those entrusted with the mysteries God has revealed. ² Now it is required that those who have been given a trust must prove faithful. ³ I care very little if I am judged by you or by any human court; indeed, I do not even judge myself. ⁴ My conscience is clear, but that does not make me innocent. It is the Lord who judges me. ⁵ Therefore judge nothing before the appointed time; wait until the Lord comes. He will bring to light what is hidden in darkness and will expose the motives of the heart. At that time each will receive their praise from God.
>
> 1 Corinthians 4:1–5

1. Circle each time Paul uses the word *judge* or *judged*. Based on these verses, what was Paul describing when he talked about judging or being judged?

2. Look at verse 2. What does it mean to be faithful in our efforts to love God and others?

3. Paul mentions "the motives of the heart" in verse 5. Use the space below to make a list of some of the good works that you've done over the past week—actions that would cause others to applaud you and approve of you. Then write down your *motives* for each of those actions. Why did you do what you did?

4. In what ways have you recently allowed yourself to judge the actions or motives of other people?

5. Read 1 Corinthians 6:1–6, which also addresses this idea of judging others. How does Paul's message in those verses complement his instructions here in 1 Corinthians 4:1–5?

6. What is one step you can take this week to choose humility rather than judgment in your everyday life?

Day 4

PUT IT INTO PRACTICE

Are you ready for a bit more challenging exercise? Below are four scenarios that you could encounter during a typical week. *Warning* . . . these situations could potentially cause Christians to feel offended, or shocked, or scandalized. Are you ready to risk it? If so, choose one of these scenarios, circle it, and then work through the questions and instructions that follow.

- You invite a new neighbor over for dinner, and he peppers his conversation with an extreme amount of profanity and dirty jokes.
- One of your child's teachers invites him or her to a school club that you consider inappropriate and even harmful.
- You are dining at a public restaurant when a group of protesters enters the building and demands that everyone inside verbally affirm their protest.
- One of your coworkers has a regular habit of loudly and rudely condemning Christians as hypocrites who are destroying the fabric of society.

1. How do you think someone would respond to your chosen scenario if he or she was self-righteous and easily offendable? Or, to put it another way, how would a modern-day Pharisee respond?

2. How do you think someone would respond to your chosen scenario if he or she was *un*offendable?

3. Now for some more honesty: How would you have responded to your chosen scenario if it happened yesterday? What would you have done?

4. Imagine your chosen scenario happens tomorrow. How would you like to respond in that moment? What specific actions or attitudes do you want to present in such a situation?

5. Let's focus for a moment on the concept of humility, which in many ways is the antidote for being judgmental. Use the space below to write down three steps you can take to demonstrate humility this week—three practical ways that you can be humble that are not dependent on what other people do or say. Here goes:

Action step 1:

Action step 2:

Action step 3:

6. Finish by connecting with someone from your group. Call, meet for coffee, engage in a meaningful text conversation, or whatever method of communication works for you. Talk through your answers to questions 1–5 with that person, and then listen as he or she does the same. Commit to praying for each other and ask the Holy Spirit to fill each of you with greater humility. Write down your reflections and takeaways after that conversation.

Day 5

CATCH UP AND READ AHEAD

Use this time to go back and complete any of the study and reflection questions from previous days this week that you weren't able to finish. Make a note below of any revelations you've had and reflect on any growth or personal insights you've gained.

Spend the next two days reading chapters 9, 10, 12, and 14 of *Unoffendable*. Use the space below to make note of anything in the chapters that stands out to you or encourages you.

WEEK 3

BEFORE GROUP MEETING	Read chapters 9, 10, 12, and 14 in *Unoffendable* Read the Welcome section (page 59)
GROUP MEETING	Discuss the Connect questions Watch the video teaching for session 3 Discuss the questions that follow as a group Do the closing exercise and pray (pages 59–67)
PERSONAL STUDY – DAY 1	Complete the daily study (pages 70–74)
PERSONAL STUDY – DAY 2	Complete the daily study (pages 75–77)
PERSONAL STUDY – DAY 3	Complete the daily study (pages 78–81)
PERSONAL STUDY – DAY 4	Complete the daily study (pages 82–84)
PERSONAL STUDY – DAY 5 (before week 4 group meeting)	Read chapters 11, 13, 15, and 16 in *Unoffendable* Complete any unfinished personal studies (page 85)

THE PHYSIO-LOGICAL EFFECTS OF ANGER

"Come to me, all you who are weary and burdened, and I will give you rest. Take my yoke upon you and learn from me, for I am gentle and humble in heart, and you will find rest for your souls. For my yoke is easy and my burden is light."

MATTHEW 11:28-30

whaT is even Happening

WELCOME | READ ON YOUR OWN

We are all becoming *something*. It might be hideous. It might be beautiful. But we're becoming something.

I hope this session is helpful. I really wanted to lay out the genius of Jesus and how his way of radical forgiveness actually shapes us.

And not just spiritually, but also physically.

His way is better. He doesn't just know how humans *think*. He knows how we *thrive*.

CONNECT | 15 MINUTES

Get the session started by choosing one of the following questions to discuss as a group:

- What is a key insight or takeaway from last week's personal study that you would like to share with the group?

  — *or* —

- On a scale of 1 (low) to 10 (high), how would you rate your stress level at about 3 o'clock in the afternoon of a typical day? Explain your response.

WATCH | 20 MINUTES

Now watch the video for this session. As you watch, use the following outline to record any thoughts or concepts that stand out to you.

I. The stress that we experienced when we feel threatened is supposed to be a *temporary* thing.

   A. There are physiological changes that happen to our bodies when we feel threatened—elevated blood pressure, cortisol level spikes, increase in adrenaline, and the like. But these changes are supposed to last only thirty seconds or so and then be over.

B. Human beings are the only creatures that hold on to these stressors, which leads to long term consequences—weight gain, skin changes, heart problems, diabetes down the line.

C. Robert Sapolsky, a primate neuroendrocrinologist at Stanford University, concludes that we should be like the animals and not get stressed out about things that *might* happen to us.

II. There are physical and relational benefits to quickly getting rid of anger.

A. We become a kind of caricature as we grow older. If we hold on to peace, we are seen as peaceful. If we hold on to anger, we are seen as bitter and angry.

B. This is why it is important *now* for us to change our lives and become different kinds of people—to actually let people off the hook in light of what God has done for us.

III. The issue of letting go of anger is centrally about trusting in God.

    A. Most of the anger and anxiety we hold onto boils down to an issue of not trusting God.

    B. A better way to live is to trust that God will deliver us and will execute his justice.

    C. If we trust in God as the "driver" of our lives, we don't have to worry about where we are going.

IV. Life becomes much easier when we choose not to be offended by people who are broken.

    A. Much like Aibileen said to Miss Hilly in the movie *The Help,* it's just tiring to continue holding on to our self-righteousness. It's such a relief to just trust God and let it go.

    B. Instead of reacting in anger when someone is being rude or talking badly to us, we can return a kind word and actually ask God to *bless* the person.

    C. The Bible says that when we do this—respond to the person in kindness—our gentle answer will turn away both their wrath and our own wrath.

DISCUSS | 35 MINUTES

Take some time to discuss what you just watched by answering the following questions. There are some suggested questions below to help you begin your discussion, but feel free to use any of the additional questions as well as time allows.

SUGGESTED QUESTIONS

1. We began this session with the statement that Jesus is the smartest man who ever lived. How do you respond to that thought? Why is the way Jesus showed us to live so genius?

2. It's easy to see the connection between anger and stress in people. Those who deal with a lot of anger and choose to hold onto it typically also feel very stressed. What are some ways you have experienced that connection between anger and stress, or stress and anger?

3. As a reminder, the message of this study is not that we should never get angry. Rather, it's that we should stop *holding on to anger*—stop carrying it with us. How have you been impacted physically during seasons of high anger and/or stress?

4. In the teaching, we also referenced a connection between anger and a lack of trust in God. When we don't trust God, we are more likely to carry anger because of all the stuff happening we don't like. How do we reverse that cycle and gain trust in God?

ADDITIONAL QUESTIONS

 5. One of the problems we have with anger is that it comes so naturally to us. When people treat us poorly, or when someone directs anger our way, it's natural to respond in kind. Who in your life is a good model of responding to anger with kindness and compassion?

6. Getting rid of anger is easier said than done, even when we understand the physical harm that anger can cause. When was a time that you were able to let go of anger? How were you ultimately able to let go of anger in that situation?

7. We become a "caricature" of what we hold on to in our lives. Carrying anger doesn't just impact us in the present moment but also influences who we become in the future. What are some words you would like people to use when describing you ten years from now?

8. We need to trust God as the "driver" of our lives. What twists and turns have you experienced recently? How have those moments impacted your ability to trust God?

RESPOND | 10 MINUTES

Jesus once told his followers, "My yoke is easy and my burden is light" (Matthew 11:30). We tend to focus on the second part of the verse, because we like the idea of burdens being light. Also, we aren't as familiar with yokes today as they were in the first century.

In Jesus' day, the obvious definition for *yoke* was a wooden thing that farmers placed on the neck of oxen to keep them in line during plowing. So, most of those yokes were big, heavy, and cumbersome. Not easy at all. But the second definition of *yoke* had to do with religious teachers. Each rabbi had a set of teachings that he wanted his disciples to follow, which was also called a *yoke*. Most rabbis had heavy yokes—their disciples had to memorize huge portions of Scripture, they were forbidden from engaging in certain recreational activities, many were not allowed to get married, and so on.

Jesus had his own yoke that he called his disciples to follow—his own expectations for how they should live and work and interact with the world. But his yoke was easy and light. It produced rest and peace rather than stress and strain. So let's take a closer look at the passage in which Jesus talks about this yoke. Have a volunteer in the group read these verses out loud, and then discuss the questions that follow.

> [25] At that time Jesus said, "I praise you, Father, Lord of heaven and earth, because you have hidden these things from the wise and learned, and revealed them to little children. [26] Yes, Father, for this is what you were pleased to do.
>
> [27] "All things have been committed to me by my Father. No one knows the Son except the Father, and no one knows the Father except the Son and those to whom the Son chooses to reveal him.
>
> [28] "Come to me, all you who are weary and burdened, and I will give you rest. [29] Take my yoke upon you and learn from me, for I am gentle and humble in heart, and you will find rest for your souls. [30] For my yoke is easy and my burden is light."
>
> Matthew 11:25–30

What specific statements did Jesus make about himself in these verses?

What are some of the reasons people feel "weary and burdened" in today's world?

In this session, we've looked at some obstacles that prevent us from trusting God. How do these verses present reasons or ways to overcome those obstacles?

PRAY | 10 MINUTES

Bring your gathering to a close by talking with God together as a group. Consider speaking openly with God about the ways you have been impacted physically and emotionally because of stress and anger. Affirm your desire to trust God and your desire to experience the rest that Jesus promised. Use the space below to write down any requests mentioned so that you and your group members can continue to pray about them in the week ahead.

Name   Request

Personal

STUDY

As we have discussed in this study, all human beings are broken and struggle with sin. This includes you, and it also includes every person you interact with every day. That brokenness is the source of a lot of anger in our lives—both giving and receiving.

In this session, we are taking a deeper look at how that anger affects us physically. Because it does affect us! We may think that we are strong enough or immune to so-called "emotional issues," but choosing to hold on to anger will always have an impact on our lives. Just as importantly, choosing to live with anger shows our lack of trust in God. Both of those realities can result in serious harm—not only physiologically, but also spiritually.

We will explore this key theme together during the next few days. You will have a chance to reflect on your own thoughts and opinions on the matters, plus see what God's Word has to say. Then you will work with a partner in your group to make a plan for responding in a way that's appropriate (and healthy) when you are tempted to hold on to anger. Before you begin, if you are reading *Unoffendable* alongside this study, you might want to take a few moments to review chapters 9, 10, 12, and 14 in the book.

SCAVENGER 📷 HUNT

The backdrop for this week's video was a jungle, complete with fake plants and an inflatable zebra. In keeping with this theme, your task is to find the most interesting stuffed animal that you can and send a picture of it to your group. It could be a stuffed lion, a tiger, a bear . . . whatever represents the jungle theme. Extra credit goes to the most interesting stuffed toy.

Day 1

LOOK FOR CUES

There are several physiological cues connected to anger. We've already mentioned the idea of "blood boiling." Anger is often associated with feelings of heat, whether in our cheeks, our forehead, the back of the neck, and so on. Other physiological cues include clenched fists, squinted eyes, snarling lips, rapid breathing, and a thumping heart. Those are the physiological effects of anger of which we are most aware—the ones that register on the surface. But it's the other effects, the ones below the surface, that cause the most damage. Let's review what we explored in the group portion of this session. In the process, you will be given the chance to review your own physiological response to the emotion of anger.

1. Think back to what you experienced during the group portion of this session—watching the videos, discussing the questions, processing the material. How did you feel at the end of that session? Use the space below to create your own personal emoji (happy face, sad face, winky face, whatever) that illustrates your state of mind as you left that group gathering.

2. You will be halfway through this study when you complete the personal study section for this session. Up to this point, what has surprised you most from this experience? Why?

What new information have you learned?

3. Read the excerpt below from chapter 12 of *Unoffendable*, and then answer the questions that follow.

> There just aren't lots of references to anger in the Bible as something wonderful. And yet we're now told it's a "gift," for our use when we feel it's "reasonable."
>
> We're also told we should be aroused to anger when we see one of God's commands being broken. Really? Then we're going to be busy . . . really, really busy. We're also going to be really, really angry, all the time—and that's just at *ourselves*, for starters.
>
> Maybe I'm supposed to be angry that often, and maybe it's really a gift. Maybe it'll make my life more joyful and peaceful . . . so long as I don't also mind the burning, blazing, cloud-bursting, striking, thundering, hailing, tearing, piercing, trampling, slaughtering, boiling, and the occasional blasting.
>
> If this is, in fact, what we're supposed to do—experience "righteous anger" whenever we're made aware of one of God's commands being broken—we'll be precisely what the world doesn't need and largely believes we already are: a bunch of uptight, seething hypocrites.
>
> The Bible directs us to get rid of anger (see Ephesians 4:31; Colossians 3:8), but the idea of "righteous anger" turns that directive on its head: we can actually pat ourselves on the back for being offended and embracing anger.
>
> And all that boiling, piercing, corrosive power becomes part of our lives—and destroys us.[8]

The phrase "corrosive power" is an especially helpful picture for anger—something that disintegrates or decays from the inside out. When have you experienced the corrosive power of holding on to strong emotions in general?

How have you specifically experienced the corrosive power of anger in your life?

4. We have taken a critical look at the concept of "righteous anger" throughout these pages. But now it's your turn. In your own words, how would you define that concept? What is it, and what does it look like during the course of a normal day?

How would you summarize your personal beliefs about righteous anger? Is it ever appropriate for people to express? If so, when? (In what specific circumstances?)

5. Read the excerpt below from chapter 9 of *Unoffendable*, and then answer the questions that follow.

> If I get to determine whether my anger is righteous or not, I'm in trouble. So are you. The reason: we can't trust ourselves.
>
> "Trust in yourself" sounds like a perfectly normal thing to do. Problem is, for the believer, it isn't biblical at all. We are deceptive to the core: "The heart is deceitful above all things, and desperately sick; who can understand it?" (Jeremiah 17:9 ESV).
>
> Or try this: "There is a way that seems right to a man, but its end is the way to death" (Proverbs 14:12 ESV).
>
> That's a far cry from "trust in yourself," as is this: "Trust in the LORD with all your heart, and lean not on your own understanding; in all your ways acknowledge Him, and He shall direct your paths. Do not be wise in your own eyes; fear the LORD and depart from evil" (Proverbs 3:5–7 NKJV).
>
> We struggle with trusting God to mete out justice. We're afraid he *won't* mete out justice, that people won't get what they deserve. So perhaps our entitlement to anger is our little way of making sure some measure of "justice" is served.
>
> We are too good at deceiving ourselves to know if we have "righteous anger" or not. Maybe this is why there is no such allowance in Scripture. Even so, we can fool ourselves into thinking we're innocent, or justified, or victimized.[9]

What are some of the ways that God has shown himself to be worthy of your trust? Take three minutes to contemplate that question, and then use the space below to write down everything that comes to mind.

Here's a more uncomfortable question: What are some of the ways you have proven that you can't trust yourself with something as powerful as anger? Contemplate that question for three minutes, and then write down everything that comes to mind.

6. Find a video of something you know will make you feel angry. (Not enraged or furious—just a little angry.) It could be a clip of your favorite sports team losing a game, or a speech from a politician you don't like, or even a commercial for a product that irritates you. As you watch, use the space below to record specific physical sensations you experience—flushed cheeks, scowling, and the like. How does your body respond when you get angry?

What are some physical symptoms you experience when you feel enraged or furious?

Day 2

DON'T BORROW
FROM TOMORROW

This week, we looked at the idea of "borrowing from tomorrow" as a source of anxiety in our lives. We often choose to worry about things that haven't happened yet. Worse yet, we often worry about things that may not happen at all. The key word here is *choose*. Emotions like worry and anxiety and stress—and, yes, even anger—are a choice.

Not at first, of course. When something bad or unexpected happens, most of us don't mentally pause for a moment and decide we're going to get angry about it. Those initial bursts of emotion are reactionary. They are responses to stimuli, either external or internal.

But . . . what happens next is our choice. We can choose to embrace those emotions and carry them as part of our lives or as part of our identity. Or we can choose to get rid of them. This is exactly what Jesus taught in the following passage:

[25] "Therefore I tell you, do not worry about your life, what you will eat or drink; or about your body, what you will wear. Is not life more than food, and the body more than clothes? [26] Look at the birds of the air; they do not sow or reap or store away in barns, and yet your heavenly Father feeds them. Are you not much more valuable than they? [27] Can any one of you by worrying add a single hour to your life?

[28] "And why do you worry about clothes? See how the flowers of the field grow. They do not labor or spin. [29] Yet I tell you that not even Solomon in all his splendor was dressed like one of these. [30] If that is how God clothes the grass of the field, which is here today and tomorrow is thrown into the fire, will he not much more clothe you—you of little faith? [31] So do not worry, saying, 'What shall we eat?' or 'What shall we drink?' or 'What shall we wear?' [32] For the pagans run after all these things, and your heavenly Father knows that you need them. [33] But seek first his kingdom and his righteousness, and all these things will be given to you as well. [34] Therefore do not worry about tomorrow, for tomorrow will worry about itself. Each day has enough trouble of its own."

Matthew 6:25-34

1. Underline each of the commands that Jesus gives in this passage above. What emotions do you experience when you read those commands?

2. Circle any word in this passage that Jesus identifies as a source of worry. Which of those circled words cause the most worry or stress or anxiety in your life?

3. What evidence do you see in Jesus' words that holding onto worry and stress is a choice?

4. Look at verse 32. Why do you think Jesus mentions "the pagans" here? What are we choosing to trust in if we are not choosing to trust in God?

5. Now look at verse 33. Seeking God and his kingdom first is something we talk about at church. But what does it *really* mean to seek first God's kingdom and his righteousness?

6. Read verse 34 three times out loud. How are you currently borrowing trouble from tomorrow in ways that produce worry and anger today?

Day 3

CHOOSE TO TRUST

We have seen that holding onto corrosive emotions such as anger, worry, and anxiety is a choice. It's something we decide to do that causes us harm, both psychologically and physiologically. It is for this reason that God told us to let those emotions go—to get rid of them.

Trusting God is also a choice. In this case, it's something we decide to do that produces benefits, both psychologically and physiologically. Choosing to trust God allows us not only to get rid of anger but also to actively experience rest, peace, fulfillment, and joy. This concept is spelled out several times in Scripture.

The group portion of this session described Jesus' promise of rest for our souls. Now let's take a look at the wisdom of Solomon on this subject. Read the following passage three times, and then work through the questions that follow.

> ³ Let love and faithfulness never leave you;
>   bind them around your neck,
>   write them on the tablet of your heart.
>
> ⁴ Then you will win favor and a good name
>   in the sight of God and man.
>
> ⁵ Trust in the Lord with all your heart
>   and lean not on your own understanding;
> ⁶ in all your ways submit to him,
>   and he will make your paths straight.
>
> ⁷ Do not be wise in your own eyes;
>   fear the Lord and shun evil.
> ⁸ This will bring health to your body
>   and nourishment to your bones.
>
> Proverbs 3:3–8

1. What phrases stand out to you in this passage? Why?

2. According to verse 2, you should write love and faithfulness "on the tablet of your heart." Use the space below to do just that. Write down some of the ways you experience God's love and faithfulness in your life.

3. Reread verse 5. How can you tell when you are leaning on your own understanding rather than trusting God?

4. When have you made the decision to trust God even though you didn't understand everything that was happening—or even when you didn't like the direction your circumstances were taking you? What happened next?

5. In verse 6, you are instructed, "in all your ways submit to him." What is one step you can take today to actively and intentionally submit to God and his will?

6. One of the rewards of trusting God is "health to your body and nourishment to your bones" (verse 8). How have you experienced these benefits in your life? Make a list of ten benefits below that you have recieved from trusting in God.

1.	2.
3.	4.
5.	6.
7.	8.
9.	10.

How would you *like* to experience these benefits to a greater degree in your life?

Day 4

PRACTICE MAKES PERFECT

They say practice makes perfect, which is true in many ways. When we actively practice a new skill or behavior, we have a better chance of mastering that skill or behavior. This is true for both positive and negative behaviors. It's entirely possible to practice making the wrong decisions. But it's also possible to practice the right decisions. When we reject opportunities to change or improve, we are actually "making perfect" our status quo. We are passively choosing not to change. So, let's actively practice something positive as we bring this session to a close.

1. Call or meet up with a person from your small group. Spend a few minutes talking through your reactions to the personal study material in this session. What have you learned? What surprised you? What made you most uncomfortable?

2. Next, work together to identify three scenarios in your community that would be fertile ground for anger. For example, a contentious parent/teacher conference, a traffic accident, a political protest. Write down those three scenarios below.

Scenario 1:

Scenario 2:

Scenario 3:

3. In your experience, what are some effective ways to return a gentle word or respond graciously when other people lash out in anger? What might that look like?

4. Now it's time to practice. Take turns with your partner playing out the scenarios you identified above. Have one person make angry or accusatory statements based on that scenario and the other respond in ways that are gentle or gracious. Switch back and forth, with each person playing the aggressor several times. Use the space below to take notes about what you find interesting or surprising during that experience.

5. What are some situations you expect in the next month that will provide opportunities for anger? (When are you likely to feel angry or encounter anger in the near future?)

6. This week, what are three ways you can continue practicing the art of using gentleness and grace to turn away the anger of others?

Way 1:

Way 2:

Way 3:

Day 5

CATCH UP AND READ AHEAD

Use this time to go back and complete any of the study and reflection questions from previous days this week that you weren't able to finish. Make a note below of any revelations you've had and reflect on any growth or personal insights you've gained.

Spend the next two days reading chapters 11, 13, 15, and 16 of *Unoffendable*. Use the space below to make note of anything in the chapters that stands out to you or encourages you.

WEEK 4

BEFORE GROUP MEETING	Read chapters 11, 13, 15, and 16 in *Unoffendable* Read the Welcome section (page 89)
GROUP MEETING	Discuss the Connect questions Watch the video teaching for session 4 Discuss the questions that follow as a group Do the closing exercise and pray (pages 89–97)
PERSONAL STUDY – DAY 1	Complete the daily study (pages 100–103)
PERSONAL STUDY – DAY 2	Complete the daily study (pages 104–106)
PERSONAL STUDY – DAY 3	Complete the daily study (pages 107–109)
PERSONAL STUDY – DAY 4	Complete the daily study (pages 110–112)
PERSONAL STUDY – DAY 5 (before week 5 group meeting)	Read chapters 17–20 in *Unoffendable* Complete any unfinished personal studies (page 113)

WHAT ABOUT INJUS- TICE?

"Wash and make yourselves clean. Take your evil deeds out of my sight; stop doing wrong. Learn to do right; seek justice. Defend the oppressed. Take up the cause of the fatherless; plead the case of the widow."

ISAIAH 1:16–17

WELCOME | READ ON YOUR OWN

This session tackles an incredibly important and often-asked question: *What about injustice?* Aren't we supposed to be angry about it?

Totally fair question.

Various podcasts/radio shows have asked me to be a guest to talk about *Unoffendable* while expecting to blast my ideas about "righteous anger" by discussing the need for anger to address injustices.

Sadly, I find they haven't actually read the book or considered my arguments. The conversation usually turns from what had planned to be a full-on argument into a conversation that goes a different direction entirely.

Can it really be true that we can address injustice without anger? I believe the answer is yes. In fact, I believe we can address injustice much *better* without it.

CONNECT | 15 MINUTES

Get the session started by choosing one of the following questions to discuss as a group:

- What is a key insight or takeaway from last week's personal study that you would like to share with the group?

  — or —

- What are the first ideas or images that come to your mind when you hear the word *justice*? Explain your response.

WATCH | 20 MINUTES

Now watch the video for this session. As you watch, use the following outline to record any thoughts or concepts that stand out to you.

I. *What about injustice?* This is a fundamental question that we must ask when it comes to considering this idea of being unoffendable.

    A. Aren't we supposed to get angry about injustice? Biblically, the answer is no. What we're supposed to do is actually *do* something about it.

    B. The examples of Dietrich Bonhoeffer and Dr. Martin Luther King, Jr. reveal that it is better for us to respond to injustice with a clear head rather than being clouded by anger.

    C. We don't want those responsible for administering justice in our society to be clouded by anger. As Dallas Willard said, "Whatever you can do with anger, you can do better without it."

II. Anger does not lead to action about injustice but to *inaction.*

    A. We call our anger "righteous" because it always seems righteous to us. We rationalize that if we are really angry we must be really righteous, because our anger is righteous!

    B. Our culture has made this error. Studies show that posts on social media that are inspiring and profound get few likes. But if you affirm someone else's anger . . . bam, it retweets and is off.

    C. Other studies show that the people who tweet the most about an issue are the least likely to give to that issue. They believe that expressing outrage is actually doing something about it.

III. There is a way to stand up for injustice without giving into anger.

    A. Letting go of anger doesn't mean we roll over or refuse to fight. It just means that we refuse to be driven by anger in that fight.

    B. The story about Brant "crashing" the press conference reveals that you can stand up for injustice without becoming clouded by rage.

    C. But if we think our anger is righteous, we not only suffer physiologically, but we can easily get deluded into believing we are taking action about an injustice.

IV. There is also a way to forgive others while still standing up for justice.

    A. When we forgive others, we demonstrate our trust in God's justice. However, this is not to minimize, mitigate, or excuse what the other person has done to us.

B. The story of Sokreaksa Himm demonstrates that we can extend forgiveness in even the most horrific situations. When we grasp the weight of God's grace toward us, we realize that we don't really have a choice in extending forgiveness—regardless of what has happened.

C. Forgiveness is radical. This is discipleship itself. This requires amazing grace. The world is broken, but we can be agents of forgiveness even as we stand against injustice.

DISCUSS | 35 MINUTES

Take some time to discuss what you just watched by answering the following questions. There are some suggested questions below to help you begin your discussion, but feel free to use any of the additional questions as well as time allows.

SUGGESTED QUESTIONS

1. Injustice is a concept that can be difficult to pin down because people have different opinions of what is right and wrong or appropriate and inappropriate. In your mind, what are some clear-cut examples of injustice in our world?

2. Contrary to popular opinion, anger does nothing to address injustice. When have you seen injustice addressed in a way that produced a solution or resolution?

3. One of the key points from this week's teaching is that anger clouds our judgment when we are attempting to deal with injustice. Where do you see examples of anger making problems worse in the world today? In your own experiences?

4. There is a great deal of confusion in the church today about the concept of forgiveness, as many believe that forgiving someone means pretending that everything is okay. What is a practical and biblical definition of what it means to actually extend forgiveness?

ADDITIONAL QUESTIONS

5. Some people seem to have a natural ability to stay calm in every situation. Who has been an example in your life of remaining cool and confident even in the most difficult situations?

6. Negative emotions are reflected and expanded on social media far more quickly than positive emotions. As a group, do a quick experiment. Browse through some social media feeds and read out loud posts or comments that express or affirm anger. Collectively, what impact do those posts have on you as you hear them?

7. Read James 4:17. It's easy to fall into the mindset that expressing anger about an injustice—like many people do on social media—equates to taking action about an injustice. What does this verse say about the need to actually *act* on what we know needs to be done?

8. Some wrongs can feel almost impossible to forgive. What objections have come to your mind during this session? In other words, what issues or circumstances seem so wrong—so unjust—that they feel like they require an angry response?

RESPOND | 10 MINUTES

There are some questions and concerns about modern life that don't have direct answers in Scripture. *How much screen time should I give my kids each day? How much should I invest in retirement savings every year? What steps should I take to balance my desire to be a good steward of my resources alongside my desire to be a good steward of the environment?*

Sure, there are principles in the Bible that address those issues and help us find solutions. But there's not a direct connection. However, that is not the case when it comes to issues such as vengeance, rage, and wrath. On *those* topics, God has made his will abundantly clear. He has told us exactly what he wants us to do. Which means the only thing up for debate is whether we will obey. Here is an example. Have a volunteer read these words from Paul out loud, and then discuss the questions that follow.

> [17] Do not repay anyone evil for evil. Be careful to do what is right in the eyes of everyone. [18] If it is possible, as far as it depends on you, live at peace with everyone. [19] Do not take revenge, my dear friends, but leave room for God's wrath, for it is written: "It is mine to avenge; I will repay," says the Lord. [20] On the contrary: "If your enemy is hungry, feed him; if he is thirsty, give him something to drink. In doing this, you will heap burning coals on his head." [21] Do not be overcome by evil, but overcome evil with good.
>
> Romans 12:17–21

What commands does God give to his followers in these verses?

When have you experienced the futility of repaying evil for evil? Conversely, when have you been successful at loving your enemy?

Where do you see opportunities in your community to overcome evil with good?

PRAY | 10 MINUTES

Close by talking with God together as a group. Spend time acknowledging the injustices present in your community and ask that God would guide and direct your group (and your church) in addressing those issues. Affirm your desire to choose forgiveness instead of anger and vengeance. Use the space below to write down any requests mentioned so that you and your group members can continue to pray about them in the week ahead.

Name   Request

Personal STUDY

In the last session, we explored the physiological effects of holding on to the anger we experience in our day-to-day lives. Carrying that anger around is corrosive. Like other forms of stress, it burns us and attacks us from the inside out—which is exactly why the Bible so often commands us to get rid of that anger!

In this session, we have been addressing the nagging questions that typically come to our minds when we consider letting go of anger for good: *But what about injustice? What about these horrible things that are happening in the world? What about the horrible things that have happened to me? Do I really just let all this go?*

As we've seen, injustice is bad enough without adding anger into the mix. There are better ways to solve the biggest problems in our culture—ways that don't include us accepting the corrosive power of anger. So, let's dive in and explore the questions of injustice and forgiveness on a deeper level over the next several days. Before you begin, if you are reading *Unoffendable* alongside this study, you might want to take a few moments to review chapters 11, 13, 15, and 16 in the book.

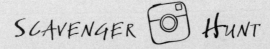

SCAVENGER 📷 HUNT

The set for this week's video teaching contained a number of traffic signs—a No Left Turn sign, a Permit Parking Only sign, a Local Traffic Only sign, and the like. So, your task this week is to take a picture of the most unique road sign that you can find. (Just be safe and don't take pictures while driving.)

Day 1

CONFRONT INJUSTICE

At this point, it's critical to stress that justice is important to God. We shouldn't walk away with the impression that injustice isn't a big deal or that followers of Jesus shouldn't be concerned about the many forms of injustice we encounter in our world. No, *injustice is a huge deal.* It is something that moves God's heart and moves him to action.

Therefore, the same should be true of us. We should take action to confront injustice wherever and whenever we can. We just don't need to get angry in order to make that happen. That is the myth we've been addressing in this session so far. So, let's keep digging into this important theme. Specifically, let's review the major concepts covered in the *Unoffendable* book and in the group study regarding this critical topic.

1. Take a look at the recent news headlines using whatever format you like best. As you skim through those headlines, where do you see real-time examples of injustice occurring in your community? In the world at large?

2. Injustice isn't something that only happens "out there" in the wider world. It's also something that we encounter as individuals. What are some ways you have encountered or endured injustice?

3. Read the excerpt below from chapter 13 of *Unoffendable*, and then answer the questions that follow.

> When talking about this with people, this idea that the Bible doesn't ever endorse human anger as a solution for injustice, I get this reaction, particularly from men: "But we've got to do something!"
>
> Yes, agreed: *Do* something. Take action.
>
> "But if we don't get angry, we won't do anything."
>
> Really? *Why?*
>
> So you can't just *do* the right thing, because it's the right thing? The Bible gives us ample commands to act, and never, ever, says to do it out of anger. Instead, we're to be motivated by something very different: love, and obedience born of love.
>
> In fact, Paul wrote in 1 Corinthians, it's the defining motivation. If we do something good, even, without love, we're just a bunch of noise (see 13:1).
>
> Acting out of love, to show mercy, to correct injustices, to set things right . . . is beautiful. Love should be motivation enough to do the right thing. And not "love" as a fuzzy abstraction, but love as a gutsy, willful decision to seek the best for others.
>
> What the world needs, I think you'll agree, is not a group of people patting themselves on the back for being angry. We need people who actually act to set things right.[10]

How would you describe the difference between *anger* and *love* as motivating factors?

When have you witnessed love driving people (or a person) to take action in the fight against injustice?

4. Let's get a little more personal. What are some examples of injustice that make you feel angry? Take three minutes and write down some examples.

Looking at the list above, draw a circle around any examples of injustice that are occurring where you live—in your city or town or community. What steps could you take to actively and intentionally fight against those examples of injustice?

5. Read the excerpt below from chapter 7 of *Unoffendable*, and then answer the questions that follow.

> But here's a bigger problem, and it's based on years of interacting with thousands of self-described Christians: It's not merely that we're not attentive to the fact that God loves us. *I suspect many of us actually just don't believe it.*
>
> I suspect this because our behavior gives us away. After all, what we believe isn't what we say we believe; it's what we do. And what many of us do, as far as I can tell, is strive and strain and push and pull and work and worry and even anguish to try to somehow win favor with a Father who's already pleased with us. I could spend an hour on the radio, reciting Scriptures about how we are now no longer under law, and how, if you've put your faith in Jesus, God has adopted you into his family, and I already know the inevitable response: Christians lined up to tell me it's not really quite true, that the real issue is that we need to stop sinning right now and work harder.
>
> No wonder we get so angry. We're displeased with others because we're convinced God is displeased with us. We "believe" God loves us, but we suspect it's provisional, based on whether we ever get our act straightened out. That's a lot to carry.

If Christians are indeed the most easily offended people on the planet, this burden would go a long way toward explaining why. We're the ones convinced God has six hundred-plus rules—rules we know we can't keep—and that he's ticked off at us. But we try to keep them anyway. It's a prescription for immense frustration with ourselves.

And then we see other people not trying as hard as we are, and that's downright enraging. We hope God will give them their comeuppance someday, because if he doesn't, what the heck are we doing all this for?[11]

We saw in a previous session that our lack of trust in God can be a source of anxiety and anger. The above quote pinpoints another source: we believe we have to earn God's love through our own efforts, which is impossible. What are some of the ways people attempt to earn God's love or prove their worthiness to him?

Where do you see the connection between feeling unloved by God and developing anger toward other people? How do those feed into each other?

6. Look back at the first question and your list that highlights examples of injustice in the world and in your community. What are some specific ways you can reflect God's love in a way that helps solve or address one of those examples?

Day 2

ADVOCATE FOR JUSTICE

It's one thing to be aware of injustice and disapprove of it—or to get angry about it. It's quite another thing to act and advocate for justice in ways that produce real change. Ultimately, that is what God has called us to do as his followers. Take action. Seek justice. Follow God's lead by taking steps to make things better.

There's an interesting moment in the Old Testament that illustrates God's desire not just to highlight injustice but also to promote justice. Speaking through the prophet Jeremiah, the Lord gives a series of powerful instructions to his people in Jerusalem prior to their defeat and destruction by the armies of Babylon.

Basically, God tells the people of Judah—from the king down—to stop playing at religion and start actually *doing something* that reflects his values. Namely, God wants his people to do justice. Read the following passage, and then answer the questions that follow.

> This is what the LORD says: "Go down to the palace of the king of Judah and proclaim this message there: [2] 'Hear the word of the LORD to you, king of Judah, you who sit on David's throne—you, your officials and your people who come through these gates. [3] This is what the LORD says: Do what is just and right. Rescue from the hand of the oppressor the one who has been robbed. Do no wrong or violence to the foreigner, the fatherless or the widow, and do not shed innocent blood in this place. [4] For if you are careful to carry out these commands, then kings who sit on David's throne will come through the gates of this palace, riding in chariots and on horses, accompanied by their officials and their people. [5] But if you do not obey these commands, declares the LORD, I swear by myself that this palace will become a ruin.'"
>
> Jeremiah 22:1–5

1. Circle any of these commands that are still relevant in today's world—any that would still create a benefit in your community and your world. Which of those commands seems most relevant to you? Why?

2. Use the space below to rewrite each of the commands contained in the verses above. What does God tell his people to do?

3. Let's take a step back and consider this concept we call *justice*. In your own words, what does it mean to "do what is just and right"? What does that look like in your everyday life?

4. When have you been involved in a just cause? Specifically, when have you taken action that reduced injustice or actively supported what was right? How have those experiences impacted your life?

5. In verse 4, God describes the rewards his people would receive if they obeyed him and actively promoted justice in their community. What rewards can we expect to enjoy for taking action to seek justice in our communities today?

6. In verse 5, God lays out the consequences his people would experience if they continued to ignore his call for justice. Where do you see negative consequences affecting the church today because of our inaction to seek justice?

Day 3

REJECT RETRIBUTION

The video teaching for this session offered a powerful quote from Rachel Denhollander, who was a victim of institutionalized abuse. Let's take another look at one of the things she said about her abuser during his trial: "I trust in God's justice and I release bitterness and anger and a desire for personal vengeance."[12]

This is the crux of what we've been exploring in this session. The world tells us that we have the right to be angry whenever we've been wronged—and that we should use that anger to seek vengeance against the person, system, or culture that wronged us. This is the concept of retribution. It's an eye for an eye. If you hurt me, I get to hurt you, and I am perfectly justified to carry my anger and bitterness and rage for as long as I choose.

As followers of Christ, we need to reject that way of thinking. We need to let go of our anger and bitterness and desire for vengeance. Why? Because we know those things will only keep us imprisoned to the past. They will harm us, not help us. For this reason, we need to reject our "right" to retribution and instead trust God to judge. Such an approach feels revolutionary in our world, but it's what Jesus commanded. Read the following passage three times, and then work through the questions that follow.

[38] "You have heard that it was said, 'Eye for eye, and tooth for tooth.' [39] But I tell you, do not resist an evil person. If anyone slaps you on the right cheek, turn to them the other cheek also. [40] And if anyone wants to sue you and take your shirt, hand over your coat as well. [41] If anyone forces you to go one mile, go with them two miles. [42] Give to the one who asks you, and do not turn away from the one who wants to borrow from you.

[43] "You have heard that it was said, 'Love your neighbor and hate your enemy.' [44] But I tell you, love your enemies and pray for those who persecute you, [45] that you may be children of your Father in heaven. He causes his sun to rise on the evil and the good, and sends rain on the righteous and the unrighteous. [46] If you love those who love you, what reward will you get? Are not even the tax collectors doing that? [47] And if you greet only your own people, what are you doing more than others? Do not even pagans do that? [48] Be perfect, therefore, as your heavenly Father is perfect.

Matthew 5:38–48

1. Take a moment to underline any commands that Jesus gave his followers in these verses. Which of those commands feels most surprising? Why?

2. The idea of an "eye for eye, and tooth for tooth" was originally meant to make punishments fair. If someone attacked you and knocked out your tooth, you didn't get to retaliate and knock out *all* that person's teeth—just the one. Using the scale below, how would you rate the fairness of punishments and conse-quences in today's culture?

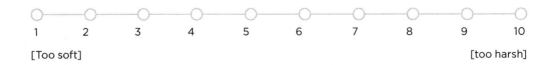

1   2   3   4   5   6   7   8   9   10

[Too soft]   [too harsh]

3. When have you recently had an opportunity to seek revenge or retribution against someone who wronged you? How did you respond?

4. How do Jesus' commands in Matthew 5:38–48 connect with this issue of anger and wrath? How do they connect with the concept of "righteous anger"?

5. We said in a previous session that forgiving others doesn't mean rolling over and ignoring the harm they have caused. How does that truth fit with Jesus' commands in verses 38–42?

6. Use the space below to write down the names of people who have harmed you or wronged you. Then, obey the commands of Jesus by praying for those people. Pray not only that God would accomplish justice but that those individuals would become aligned to his will.

Day 4

CHOOSE FORGIVENESS

Here's something we know to be true: *forgiveness is hard*. We've been talking throughout this study about the value of forgiveness, the benefits of forgiveness, and the necessity of forgiving those who wrong us. All of that is true and helpful. And yet—*forgiveness is still hard*. It is a difficult thing to do in the best of circumstances, and it feels near impossible in the worst.

In the end, though, it's necessary. Forgiveness is necessary not only because Jesus commanded us to forgive—although obviously that is hugely important—but also because forgiveness benefits us. It allows us to stop carrying anger and other emotions that are causing us harm. So, let's get practical as we move toward the conclusion of this session. Let's choose to forgive at least one person who has wronged us, and let's do it in conversation with another group member so that we can benefit from mutual encouragement and support.

1. One trick that can help you extend forgiveness to others is remembering the ways you have been forgiven in the past. Use the space below to draw a picture that represents a moment you were forgiven by someone else—a moment when you received forgiveness from another person that you did not deserve.

2. What emotions did you experience during the process of completing your drawing? What are some of the main memories that came to mind?

3. Now turn your attention to moments and memories that reflect the ways you have been wronged by others. Which of those moments have impacted you the most strongly? Write them down in the space below.

4. Looking at this list of instances where you have been harmed by others, circle any moments where you have not yet forgiven the person who wronged you. What are the main obstacles that have been holding you back and preventing you from extending forgiveness?

5. Now it's time to verbally offer forgiveness to one of the people listed above. Work through the statements below in a conversation with God. (You may need to pray through these statements several times before they "stick" in your heart.)

> Heavenly Father, I am choosing to forgive _____
> for the ways they have wronged me. I am choosing forgiveness in obedience to you and your commands.
>
> In the name of Jesus Christ, I release any negative emotions that I am carrying toward _____. I release all anger, rage, bitterness, and shame. I say no to those emotions and say yes to forgiveness.
>
> In the name of Jesus Christ, I release any desire for retribution or revenge against _____. I affirm the truth of Scripture that vengeance belongs to God alone.
>
> Heavenly Father, I submit to your justice and your will when it comes to the consequences that _____ will experience because of their actions. I trust you, God, to be the judge.

 6. Finish by calling or meeting up with a partner from your group. Share what you have experienced today and pray for one another. Specifically pray that God's Spirit would heal you from damage caused by holding on to anger and other harmful emotions. Write down your takeaways below from your conversation.

Day 5

CATCH UP AND READ AHEAD

Use this time to go back and complete any of the study and reflection questions from previous days this week that you weren't able to finish. Make a note below of any revelations you've had and reflect on any growth or personal insights you've gained.

Spend the next two days reading chapters 17–20 of *Unoffendable*. Use the space below to make note of anything in the chapters that stands out to you or encourages you.

WEEK 5

BEFORE GROUP MEETING	Read chapters 17–20 in *Unoffendable* Read the Welcome section (page 117)
GROUP MEETING	Discuss the Connect questions Watch the video teaching for session 5 Discuss the questions that follow as a group Do the closing exercise and pray (pages 117–125)
PERSONAL STUDY – DAY 1	Complete the daily study (pages 128–132)
PERSONAL STUDY – DAY 2	Complete the daily study (pages 133–135)
PERSONAL STUDY – DAY 3	Complete the daily study (pages 136–138)
PERSONAL STUDY – DAY 4	Complete the daily study (pages 139–142)
PERSONAL STUDY – DAY 5 (before week 6 group meeting)	Read chapters 21–24 in *Unoffendable* Complete any unfinished personal studies (page 143)

HOW TO ACTU-ALLY DO THIS

"A new command I give you: Love one another. As I have loved you, so you must love one another. By this everyone will know that you are my disciples, if you love one another."

JOHN 13:34-35

SOMETHING BEAUTIFUL
IS ABOUT TO HAPPEN

WELCOME | READ ON YOUR OWN

There are many people who write to me, after they've read *Unoffendable*, to thank me for the book and then say, "But this is so hard! I have to keep practicing this!"

And I agree with them, of course. Because I'm still practicing it myself. This is what it means to pick up our crosses daily. There's a sacrifice we are making; we're nailing our own self-righteousness to a tree, and we're doing it to honor a God who has done that for us.

No, forgiveness is not easy. But it's *far* easier than a life of unforgiveness.

In this session, we will also see how it's also much more enjoyable. We begin to not just love people more but even to *like* them as well. We see how precious people really are.

They're works of art, by our favorite artist.

CONNECT | 15 MINUTES

Get the session started by choosing one of the following questions to discuss as a group:

- What is a key insight or takeaway from last week's personal study that you would like to share with the group?

  — *or* —

- On a scale of 1 (very little) to 10 (very much), to what degree do you worry about what other people think of you? Explain your response.

WATCH | 20 MINUTES

Now watch the video for this session. As you watch, use the following outline to record any thoughts or concepts that stand out to you.

I. The more you become unoffendable, the more you will be willing to forgive people as a lifestyle.

    A. You won't be looking for something in people to be disgusted about or be scandalized by them. Instead, you will start to look for things in them that maybe other people don't see.

    B. You will start to look at people like artists look at things. You will develop a different way of seeing things that allows you to see the value of people.

    C. You will be willing to "move the fence" and accept those you might have previously excluded.

II. Viewing people through the lens of forgiveness means seeing them in the way that God sees us.

    A. One of the wonderful things about being unoffendable is that it frees us up to be less fearful—and be our true selves—because we don't care what everybody thinks about us anymore.

B. There is something about practicing this kind of radical forgiveness that lowers the stakes in our relationships. If other people don't like us . . . it's okay. If we make fools out of ourselves . . . it's okay. We're just doing the next thing that God puts in front of us . . . and God honors our efforts.

C. The beauty of becoming unoffendable is that people begin to pick up on the fact that we not only *love* them . . . but that we actually *like* them.

III. The only thing that allows us to transcend arguments and differing opinions is relationships.

A. Behavioral psychologists tell us that we are not rational beings. We are *emotional* beings. We use our rationality to back up what we already want to believe.

B. For this reason, it is very difficult for people to change their minds about anything. Arguments on social media *never* work because it just degenerates into people yelling at each other.

C. The only thing that has been proven to change people's minds are *relationships*. When we know another person, and know that person cares about us, we will be open to their opinions.

IV. It is our job as followers of Christ to make it plausible for people to believe that God loves them.

A. We demonstrate to others that God loves them by the way that we live our lives.

B. We embrace forgiveness by putting Calvary at the end of our thoughts—not at the front. Instead of saying, "Yeah, Calvary happened . . . but they did this," we say, "Yeah, they did this . . . but Calvary happened."

DISCUSS | 35 MINUTES

Take some time to discuss what you just watched by answering the following questions. There are some suggested questions below to help you begin your discussion, but feel free to use any of the additional questions as time allows.

SUGGESTED QUESTIONS

1. Artists have a natural ability to look at something that seems rough on the surface and understand its true potential. In what ways is this like living an unoffendable lifestyle?

2. Part of becoming unoffendable means no longer viewing forgiveness as a case-by-case option. In other words, you no longer pick and choose what person or what offenses you will forgive but instead extend forgiveness to everyone. Who is someone in your life who has modeled this for you? What strikes you most about their ability to forgive?

3. Living in a lifestyle of forgiveness is counter-cultural. It goes against our basic human instincts and reactions. In your experience, what have been the biggest obstacles that have hindered you from viewing the world through the lens of radical forgiveness?

4. When you genuinely love people, you find it much easier to forgive their brokenness—and they find it much easier to let down their guard and connect with you. What does it mean on a practical level to "love" others? What does that look like in your life?

ADDITIONAL QUESTIONS

5. Think of your life in terms of a home renovation show on TV. What are some of the biggest ways you have grown and matured in recent years? Where do you still need some work?

6. Ask someone in the group to read aloud Romans 5:8. Embracing forgiveness as a lifestyle means seeing other people the way that God sees them. So, how do you think that God sees them? What does this passage say about the depth of God's love for *all* people?

7. Behavioral psychologists tell us that humans use their rationality to back up what they already believe, which is why it is so difficult to change another person's mind. How have you found this to be true? What is most effective in changing another person's mind?

8. We've been studying this idea of being unoffendable for several weeks now. In that time, how would you rate your success in letting go of anger and embracing forgiveness? If you have seen some growth in this area, how has it impacted your relationships with others?

RESPOND | 10 MINUTES

In this week's teaching, we discussed how *Calvary* should be the lens through which we always view other people. No matter how messed up or broken someone else might be, he or she is still a person for whom Jesus willingly died on the cross to save. Yes, people make mistakes. Yes, people will hurt us and wrong us in any number of ways. *But Calvary . . .*

What is fascinating is that Jesus himself was unoffendable—and he proved it at Calvary. Even nailed to a cross, he chose to view humanity through the lens of radical forgiveness, as the following passage in Luke relates. Ask a volunteer to read each of these verses out loud, and then work as a group to discuss the questions that follow.

> [32] Two other men, both criminals, were also led out with him to be executed. [33] When they came to the place called the Skull, they crucified him there, along with the criminals—one on his right, the other on his left. [34] Jesus said, "Father, forgive them, for they do not know what they are doing." And they divided up his clothes by casting lots.
>
> [35] The people stood watching, and the rulers even sneered at him. They said, "He saved others; let him save himself if he is God's Messiah, the Chosen One."
>
> [36] The soldiers also came up and mocked him. They offered him wine vinegar [37] and said, "If you are the king of the Jews, save yourself."
>
> [38] There was a written notice above him, which read: THIS IS THE KING OF THE JEWS.
>
> [39] One of the criminals who hung there hurled insults at him: "Aren't you the Messiah? Save yourself and us!"

> [40] But the other criminal rebuked him. "Don't you fear God," he said, "since you are under the same sentence? [41] We are punished justly, for we are getting what our deeds deserve. But this man has done nothing wrong."
>
> [42] Then he said, "Jesus, remember me when you come into your kingdom."
>
> [43] Jesus answered him, "Truly I tell you, today you will be with me in paradise."
>
> Luke 23:32–43

In what ways did Jesus demonstrate radical forgiveness while he was on the cross?

How can you make this kind of forgiveness work in your life? Meaning, in the moments after someone has wronged you, how can you choose to stay focused on the cross and respond appropriately?

Today's culture is full of personal attacks and group-based shaming. What opportunities do you have right now to offer a blessing to those who are attempting to insult or defame you?

PRAY | 10 MINUTES

Close your gathering by talking with God together as a group. Affirm your desire to be unoffendable—to adopt a *lifestyle* of radical forgiveness rather than forgiving a few people on an *a la carte* basis. Ask God to guide you toward specific action steps you can take this week to practice radical forgiveness. Use the space below to write down any requests mentioned so that you and your group members can continue to pray about them in the week ahead.

Name   Request

Personal STUDY

In the last session, we focused on the themes of *justice* and *injustice*. We saw that God actively cares about those issues and takes steps in our world to punish injustice and promote justice. This is why we don't need anger as a fuel to solve injustice. God is already on the job.

In this session, we've been focused on the practical side of being unoffendable. How do we actually move from offendable to unoffendable? What does it look like to get rid of anger? What steps can we take to adopt a lifestyle of radical forgiveness? These are the questions we will explore in greater detail over the next few days. But before you begin, if you are reading *Unoffendable* alongside this study, you might want to take a few moments to review chapters 17–20 in the book.

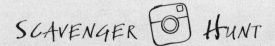

SCAVENGER HUNT

In the middle of the set for this week's teaching was a giant lobster made out of scrap metal, which illustrated the "artist's eye" in seeing the hidden potential of things that on the surface look like junk. So, your task this week is to snap a picture of an interesting piece of scrap metal or junk. Extra credit given to those who work those pieces of junk into one of the sculptures featured in the session (red lobster, eagle, grasshopper, stork, flying bird, scary face).

Day 1

TOP TEN QUALITIES

Part of being unoffendable is seeing beyond the way people speak and behave in the present moment. As you've certainly experienced, a lot of people speak and behave in ways that can make you feel angry—if you let them. People are messed up . . . and one of the realities about messed-up people is that they often do messed-up things.

Still, it is possible to see beyond that reality. In the same way that artists look at raw materials and focus on what those materials can *become*, you can look at the people in your life and see them for who they were *meant to be*. You can seek to see them as God sees them—women and men created in his image who are recipients of his grace. As you get started with the personal study portion of this session, continue to explore how you can see people through the lens of forgiveness rather than through the lens of selfishness or self-interest.

1. Use the space below to write down the name of ten of your favorite people. Next to each name, write down one or two things you like best about that person.

1.	2.
3.	4.
5.	6.

7. .	8.
9.	10.

2. Circle any qualities that are repeated among two or more people. What are specific ways you can search for those qualities in people who are not on your top-ten list?

3. Read the excerpt below from chapter 17 of *Unoffendable*, and then answer the questions that follow.

> But the King of kings wants *you* so bad he'd give up his only Son to be with you?
>
> He not only allows it, but *desires* that you and I—lowly us!—talk to him often, whenever we want?
>
> He's not asking us to try harder, but to *trust* that the work is already done to bring us into his family?
>
> He wants to spend eternity—his eternity—with us?
>
> Yes.
>
> If we're mindful of this, and if we really believe it, how does this not leave us stunned and joyful? How does it not leave us less apt to take, and keep, offense? How can we continue to so easily feel slighted and hurt?

> If we really believe it, we'll be known for being less apt to criticize, slower to anger, more forgiving. We'll be known for being loving toward one another, because we now have the resources to do just that. We've finally found what we've always wanted—significance and security, directly from the only One who can really give us both: the King of kings.
>
> *In fact, if this is true, that very love toward one another would be an accurate test of whether we really believed all this.* If we loved others with a newfound patience, a refusal to take offense, and a lack of self-seeking, it would be evidence that all this is real.
>
> The best evidence, maybe.[13]

What does it mean to "really believe" that God loves us and wants to spend time with us? What does it look like in a person's life when he or she knows that to be true?

What about you? Where do you see evidence in your life that you are confident in God's love and affection for you? Where do you see potential evidence of the contrary?

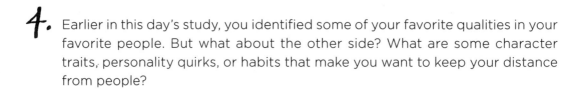

4. Earlier in this day's study, you identified some of your favorite qualities in your favorite people. But what about the other side? What are some character traits, personality quirks, or habits that make you want to keep your distance from people?

When have you been able to look past those negative elements and forge a relationship with someone who initially got on your nerves? How did it happen?

 Read the excerpt below from chapter 19 of *Unoffendable*, and then answer the questions that follow.

> It may also have been obvious to you, for a long time, that "ministry" itself—serving others—*has to involve deciding not to be offended.*
>
> It's not an option. It is the essence of ministry. It finally occurred to me that we can't be agents of healing in people's lives unless we're ready to bear their wounds for them and from them. Looking back, I wonder why it took me so long, how someone who purports to follow Jesus wouldn't have understood this.
>
> He did precisely this for us: bore our wounds, and took a beating from us, and endured our betrayals. But he was not alienated from us. The disciples who'd abandoned him looked up, and there he was, on the shore, making breakfast for them.
>
> I want to be like that. When I'm at my best, you can't offend me. When you look up, I want to still be there.
>
> This is ministry itself. I'm not sure there's another kind.[14]

How would you describe your ministry as a follower of Jesus in your community? What are some of the ways that you seek to serve God and serve others?

What role does forgiveness play in that ministry? When has it been necessary for you?

6. When it comes to forgiveness, each of us is different. What deeply offends you might warrant a shrug from someone else. So, what are the *big* offenses for you? What are the actions or attitudes that you find the most difficult to forgive? Explain your response.

Day 2

COMMANDED TO LOVE

When Jesus endured the shame and inconvenience of taking on a human body, he revealed how we should live as human beings. He engaged in all the routines, rigors, and absurdities of "normal" life so that he could show us how to do it well. He showed us how to live rightly.

When Jesus took on human flesh, he also showed us how to love one another. As he said, "'Love the Lord your God with all your heart and with all your soul and with all your mind.' This is the first and greatest commandment. And the second is like it: 'Love your neighbor as yourself'" (Matthew 22:37–39). Of course, we are good at knowing how to love ourselves—we do much of that by instinct. What's much more difficult is loving others. This is exactly where Jesus' life (and teachings) shine in our dark world.

What we need to understand in the here and now is that being unoffendable is part of what it means to love others. In fact, loving like Jesus loved—with a love that refused to be offended or hold on to grudges and was constantly ready to forgive at a moment's notice—is how the world will identify who belongs to Christ and who does not. With this in mind, read the following passage three times, and then answer the questions that follow.

> 33 "My children, I will be with you only a little longer. You will look for me, and just as I told the Jews, so I tell you now: Where I am going, you cannot come.
>
> 34 "A new command I give you: Love one another. As I have loved you, so you must love one another. 35 By this everyone will know that you are my disciples, if you love one another."
>
> 36 Simon Peter asked him, "Lord, where are you going?"
>
> Jesus replied, "Where I am going, you cannot follow now, but you will follow later."

> ³⁷ Peter asked, "Lord, why can't I follow you now? I will lay down my life for you."
>
> ³⁸ Then Jesus answered, "Will you really lay down your life for me? Very truly I tell you, before the rooster crows, you will disown me three times!"
>
> John 13:33–38

1. Jesus' central command in these verses is, "Love one another." Take three minutes and write down different actions and attitudes in the space below that seem loving to you.

2. When has someone loved you in a way that stood out—in a way that helped you understand that person was wonderfully different? Explain your response.

3. Jesus tells his disciples that he is giving them a new *command* (see verse 34). This means that loving other people is not an *option* but a *requirement* for those who belong to God's kingdom. Using the scale below, how would you rate your ability to obey that commandment recently? Has your behavior toward others been loving or unloving?

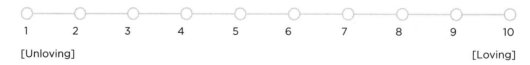

| 1 | 2 | 3 | 4 | 5 | 6 | 7 | 8 | 9 | 10 |

[Unloving]   [Loving]

4. Now take this question to the next level. Think specifically about the people you don't care for—people you would label as enemies or at least annoyances. Has your behavior toward those people been loving or unloving in recent months?

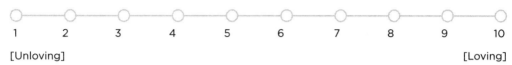

1   2   3   4   5   6   7   8   9   10

[Unloving]   [Loving]

5. Read John 21:15–19 to see what happened to Peter after the betrayal took place that Jesus mentioned above. How do Jesus' words and actions in these verses illustrate what it means to truly love others? How do they reveal what it means to forgive?

6. The theme of this session is how to actually *do* this (be unoffendable), so let's end with some action steps. What are two specific and practical steps that you can take this week to show love to those who really don't deserve it?

Action step 1:

Action step 2:

Day 3

LOVING *THOSE* PEOPLE

In yesterday's personal study, we made the case that loving other people is the hallmark of living as a follower of Christ. (Actually, Jesus made that case to his disciples some 2,000 years ago.) Given that reality, it follows that *not loving* others is a key indicator that something is wrong in our spiritual lives.

Think about it. If loving others shows that we take Jesus seriously and are serious about serving him, then refusing to love others shows the opposite. This is true even when we refuse to love *those people*. You know the ones . . . the people who really, really irritate us. Or who wronged us in the past. Or who are, right this minute, actively trying to harm us in some way.

Yes, Jesus has commanded us to even love *those* people. And when we choose to disobey that command, it reveals something about us. Something not so good. Read through the following passage twice to see the apostle Paul's take on this issue, and then work through the questions that come after.

> [1] If I speak in the tongues of men or of angels, but do not have love, I am only a resounding gong or a clanging cymbal. [2] If I have the gift of prophecy and can fathom all mysteries and all knowledge, and if I have a faith that can move mountains, but do not have love, I am nothing. [3] If I give all I possess to the poor and give over my body to hardship that I may boast, but do not have love, I gain nothing.
>
> [4] Love is patient, love is kind. It does not envy, it does not boast, it is not proud. [5] It does not dishonor others, it is not self-seeking, it is not easily angered, it keeps no record of wrongs. [6] Love does not delight in evil but rejoices with the truth. [7] It always protects, always trusts, always hopes, always perseveres.
>
> [8] Love never fails.
>
> 1 Corinthians 13:1–8

1. What caught your attention as you read these verses just now? Why?

2. When have you been hurt or derailed because of another person's lack of love?

3. Look at verses 1–3. Obviously, it's possible to take the correct action with an incorrect attitude—but how can we know? What signs or symptoms can alert us to the reality that we are trying to serve God without love?

4. Where do you see love being poured out on others from those in the church today? What about in your community?

5. Where do you see the church today in danger of going through the motions without a true love for the people they are trying to serve?

6. Here's another chance to develop some action steps. Where do you have a chance to show love to someone today? Write two options below, and then pick one to actually carry out this week.

Option 1:

Option 2:

Day 4

CREATING AN ACTION PLAN

One of the themes that has come up several times in this week's personal study is "action." When you want to resolve something or create something positive, action is way better than anger. In fact, most times, taking action is the *only* way to get something done.

So let's take action. Specifically, identify some areas of your life in which you are holding on to anger. This could be anger at God, anger at yourself, anger at others, anger at circumstances, and more. It's time to identify those sources of anger in your life. Then, it's time to let the anger go . . . to get rid of it.

Now, this is easier said than done, so we're going to walk through the process using the steps outlined below. Also, you are encouraged to connect with a fellow group member so you can work together in figuring out how to actually reject anger and choose to be unoffendable.

1. Use the space below to write down moments when you felt angry in the past few weeks. Don't include moments when you felt just irked—like when they were out of your favorite cereal at the store. Instead, write down every instance that comes to mind of when you felt truly mad, upset, wrathful, furious, seething.

2. Now write down the major causes of anger in your life. Start with the list above and identify the "why" behind your anger in those moments. But also think back to moments in your past when you felt furious. What are the biggest sources of anger in your life?

3. Now, this may sound awkward, but it's critical in this process. *Repent* of any time you held on to anger against another person. Start with the list above, but also ask the Holy Spirit to bring to mind any other time you have chosen to carry anger and hold on to it rather than letting it go. Here is a sample prayer you can use to verbally repent of holding on to anger:

> *Lord Jesus, I confess that I became filled with anger when _____.*
> *I confess that I chose to hold on to that anger. Lord, I repent of that choice. By the*
> *power of your blood that was shed on the cross, Lord Jesus, I choose to let that*
> *anger go. I reject it, I release it, and I ask that you would take it away from me.*

4. It's time to check in with your partner from the group. First, write out what has been most difficult or most surprising in this process of releasing your anger. Second, write down your next step that you will take. What is the next goal that you want to accomplish when it comes to releasing your anger?

Now, for accountability and support, talk through those items with your partner.

What has been most difficult or surprising for me?

What is the next step that I will take?

5. Pray for one another before you end your conversation. Ask that the Holy Spirit will convict you whenever you are at risk of holding on to anger. Ask that you would be filled with a deep awareness of God's forgiveness when those moments arise. Use the space below to write down anything you sense God is saying to you after spending this time in prayer.

6. Hopefully, this experience has been helpful in beginning the process of releasing any anger that you've been carrying. But remember that it is only the beginning. Now consider what steps you can build into your daily routine to identify any anger you are holding on to and then let that anger go. Use the suggestions below to come up with a plan.

How can you use your prayer life to identify and release anger?

What kinds of reminders can you set up through your phone or other devices?

How can you enlist other people to help keep you accountable?

Day 5

CATCH UP AND READ AHEAD

Use this time to go back and complete any of the study and reflection questions from previous days this week that you weren't able to finish. Make note of any revelations you've had and reflect on any growth or personal insights you've gained.

Spend the next two days reading chapters 21–24 of *Unoffendable*. Use the space below to make note of anything in the chapters that stands out to you or encourages you.

Schedule

BEFORE GROUP MEETING	Read chapters 21–24 in *Unoffendable* Read the Welcome section (page 147)
GROUP MEETING	Discuss the Connect questions Watch the video teaching for session 6 Discuss the questions that follow as a group Do the closing exercise and pray (pages 147–155)
PERSONAL STUDY – DAY 1	Complete the daily study (pages 158–162)
PERSONAL STUDY – DAY 2	Complete the daily study (pages 163–165)
PERSONAL STUDY – DAY 3	Complete the daily study (pages 166–168)
PERSONAL STUDY – DAY 4	Complete the daily study (pages 169–171)
PERSONAL STUDY – DAY 5	Finish the final session (page 172). Connect with your group about the next study that you want to go through together.

THE DIFFER-ENCE IT MAKES

"This day I call the heavens and the earth as witnesses against you that I have set before you life and death, blessings and curses. Now choose life, so that you and your children may live and that you may love the Lord your God, listen to his voice, and hold fast to him."

DEUTERONOMY 30:19-20

Nevertheless, I remain at Peace.

WELCOME | READ ON YOUR OWN

Frequently asked questions: "Seriously, do I *have* to forgive people? Do I *have* to endeavor to let go of my anger against them?"

Answer: No, you don't have to. You *get* to.

This lifestyle is a gift. You are only able to do it because it's been done for you.

And yes, while Jesus demands it of his followers, you do have the freedom to walk away. People walked away from Jesus frequently in the Gospels. It's remarkable how he didn't coerce them, or restrain them, even though he certainly could.

I hope, in this last session, you're able to reflect the whole idea of living this way—living a life of radical forgiveness. And I hope you can see how it's really about trust: trusting God with final judgment. Trusting *his* righteous anger. And trusting that his promises are true.

We know how this ends.

CONNECT | 15 MINUTES

Get the session started by choosing one of the following questions to discuss as a group:

- What is a key insight or takeaway from last week's personal study that you would like to share with the group?

  — *or* —

- When was the last time you received (or gave) a meaningful gift "just because"? Explain the situation.

WATCH | 20 MINUTES

Now watch the video for this session. As you watch, use the following outline to record any thoughts or concepts that stand out to you.

I. Being unoffendable involves constantly reminding ourselves that we don't deserve God's forgiveness—and yet God has chosen to forgive us anyway.

A. Gratitude and anger cannot coexist. Neither can thankfulness and anger. It's either one or the other, and we have to choose.

B. And we must choose wisely, for one of those will kill us, while the other will give us life.

II. We need to constantly remind ourselves of God's grace because we are forgetful.

A. We forget how good God is and how faithful he has been to us. This is why we get worried about so much stuff . . . because we forget how God has come through for us in the past.

B. God is fully aware of our forgetfulness. This is why in his Word he continually reminds us to remember, remember, remember his goodness and faithfulness (see Deuteronomy 8:2).

III. Another key to being unoffendable is to quit feeding our anger.

    A. When something (like the news) keeps pushing us into anger, we need to stop exposing ourselves to it. We can't allow ourselves to be manipulated and goaded into anger.

    B. Remember the gift Jesus promised his followers: *peace.* Do we really want to say to Jesus, "Thank you for the gift, but I would rather hold on to my anger"?

    C. Remember that forgiving others isn't dependent on an apology. More often than not, the people who wrong us are not going to apologize. We can forgive them anyway.

IV. Followers of Jesus have a ministry of reconciliation.

    A. Scholar D.A. Carson said the church is a natural band of enemies who stay together for Jesus' sake. But wouldn't it be better if we were the people who stuck together and forgave each other—and then forgave other people just as easily as breathing?

B. The world has a huge anger problem. Our anger and our stress and our anxiety are literally killing us. But as followers of Christ, we have the *solution*.

C. We are all like the baseball team that lost thirteen straight games and then had the limo show up at the end of the season. We have been given grace by God that we didn't deserve. Wouldn't it be amazing if we learned how to extend that same undeserved grace to others?

DISCUSS | 35 MINUTES

Take some time to discuss what you just watched by answering the following questions. There are some suggested questions below to help you begin your discussion, but feel free to use any of the additional questions as time allows.

SUGGESTED QUESTIONS

1. In this week's teaching, we saw that gratitude and anger cannot coexist because they are mutually exclusive. When have you experienced that reality in your life?

2. One of the reasons we feel anxious and angry about our circumstances is that we forget all the ways God has been faithful in the past—all the ways he has blessed us and provided for us. What steps can you take to keep God's faithfulness at the forefront of your mind?

3. We often fail to forgive people because we are waiting for an apology from them or waiting for some sign that they recognize they were wrong. When have you given or received forgiveness *without* an apology? What happened next?

4. Anger often feels like something automatic—something that happens instinctively. In truth, we often feed that emotion by exposing ourselves to people or things that make us angry. In what ways have you been feeding anger into your mind and heart?

ADDITIONAL QUESTIONS

5. When it comes to feeding our anger, we often have help. Where do you see organizations or elements within the culture intentionally stoking anger among people?

6. In this week's teaching, we made the case that Christians can provide the solution for the world's anger problem. How would you summarize that solution in your own words?

7. What does it mean to be a minister of reconciliation? What would it look like if everyone in the church took on this ministry of forgiving others and extending God's grace?

8. We are coming to the end of this study. How has your approach to anger and forgiveness changed during the course of the past six sessions?

RESPOND | 10 MINUTES

The book of Proverbs holds an interesting place within Christendom. Some of us view its contents like a spiritual version of a fortune cookie—interesting nuggets of insight in a pleasant-sounding package. As a result, we often don't take Proverbs as seriously as we should.

Why *should* we take it seriously? Because it's the Word of God. What we find in the wisdom literature generally—and in Proverbs specifically—is just that: *wisdom*. In particular, we find *God's* wisdom. For that reason, we should approach Proverbs not as a collection of good advice but as a distillation of God's wisdom that has direct application to our lives. With that in mind, let's take a quick look at what the book of Proverbs has to say about anger. (Oh, and the final passage below is a "proverb" pulled from the book of Ecclesiastes. So it still counts!)

A gentle answer turns away wrath, but a harsh word stirs up anger.

Proverbs 15:1

Do not make friends with a hot-tempered person,
    do not associate with one easily angered,
or you may learn their ways
    and get yourself ensnared.

Proverbs 22:24–25

Mockers stir up a city, but the wise turn away anger.

Proverbs 29:8

If you play the fool and exalt yourself,
    or if you plan evil,
    clap your hand over your mouth!
For as churning cream produces butter,
    and as twisting the nose produces blood,
    so stirring up anger produces strife.

Proverbs 30:32–33

The end of a matter is better than its beginning,
    and patience is better than pride.
Do not be quickly provoked in your spirit,
    for anger resides in the lap of fools.

Ecclesiastes 7:8–9

How would you summarize the overall sentiment of these proverbs? What do they communicate about anger?

Which of these proverbs feels most relevant to our culture right now? Why?

It's one thing to know the right thing to do and another to actually do it. What obstacles are holding you back from following God's wisdom when it comes to anger and radical forgiveness?

PRAY | 10 MINUTES

Close your time by talking with God as a group. Join together in thanking him for what you have learned and experienced in this study. As you do, be as specific as you are comfortable. Conclude by declaring your hopes and goals when it comes to living in a way that is unoffendable. Finally, use the space below to write down any requests mentioned so that you and your group members can continue to pray about them in the weeks ahead.

Name	Request

Well . . . we've reached the end! As a reminder, we've spent the last five sessions exploring what it means to be unoffendable—to live in such a way that we reject anger and embrace radical forgiveness. Hopefully, the material has been helpful for you not just in a thought-provoking way but also in terms of your everyday life.

In the previous session, we started to answer the question, *"How do we actually do this?"* We saw that choosing to be unoffendable means constantly reminding ourselves of the incredible grace and forgiveness that we have received from God. When we realize that we have been spared an incredible debt that we could never pay, we are much more likely to cancel the debts of anger, bitterness, and revenge we carry against those who wrong us.

As we conclude with this final series of personal studies, we are going to explore the benefits of becoming unoffendable. How does radical forgiveness improve our lives? How does it change who we are and what we experience? You know the drill by now! So let's get going as we conclude this study. Once again, and for the final time, if you are reading *Unoffendable* alongside this study, take a few moments to review chapters 21–24 in the book.

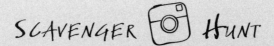

The backdrop for this week's final video teaching was a (zombie) limo driver carrying a tray. In keeping with this theme (well, not the zombie part), your final task is to take a picture of someone you respect and admire for his or her acts of service to others. This could be the wait staff at a local restaurant, the custodian at your children's school, or the person who picks up your garbage cans or delivers your mail. Just be sure to get the person's permission to take the shot!

Day 1

LIFE OR DEATH

What we've been talking about throughout this study really is a *choice*—and one that we make every day. On the one hand, we can choose to get angry whenever we feel wronged or affronted. We can choose to then carry that anger around with us so that it's available whenever we feel like gnawing on an old wound. This choice, as we have seen, leads to death. It causes harm both internally and externally, and it sets us outside of God's will for our lives.

On the other hand, we can choose to reject anger and embrace radical forgiveness. Now, this doesn't mean we'll never get angry. But it does mean we refuse to *carry* that anger around with us. We choose to get rid of it as soon as possible. This choice, as we have seen, leads to life. It leads to forgiveness, rest, and God's perfect peace.

Yes, the choice really is that simple. So what will you choose? To help you along in that decision, let's review the material we covered in the group portion of this final session.

1. When has anger or unforgiveness produced "death" in your life? Write down as many examples as you can think of in the next three minutes.

2. When has forgiveness and getting rid of anger produced "life" for you? Again, write down as many examples as come to mind in the next three minutes.

3. Read the excerpt below from chapter 23 of *Unoffendable,* and then answer the questions that follow.

> When we choose, ahead of time—before conversations, before meetings, before our day begins—to be unoffendable, we're simply choosing humility.
>
> And while, yes, anger happens, as we discussed earlier, it happens so much *less* for people whose egos are not inflamed and who have so little to lose or gain from the approval of others.
>
> Humility means there's so much less at stake, so much less to protect.
>
> You'll become difficult to offend simply because there's so much less of you to defend. When you are headed into a stressful social situation, with difficult, offensive people, and you decide in advance, "I'm not going to let these people offend me; I'm forgiving them in advance," you are dying to yourself. You are sacrificing yourself on their behalf. You are making yourself less. You're willingly giving up your own interests and desires, because of your conviction about who Jesus is.
>
> And Jesus tells us there's a reward for this: "Those who want to save their lives will give up true life, and those who give up their lives for me will have true life" (Matthew 16:25 NCV).
>
> At the beginning of this book, we talked about the crazy idea that we are not entitled to anger, and how taking this idea seriously actually opens up new dimensions of rest, grace, and simplicity in our lives. We are, above all, embracing a radical humility.
>
> We're denying ourselves, doing something seemingly self-negating, and then finding that, just as Jesus promised, we haven't lost anything. We've only gained life.[15]

Think about the next moment you are likely to experience anger—an upcoming meeting, family reunion, local sports game, and so on. What would it look like for you to "forgive those people in advance"?

Take a moment to think about that term "radical humility." What do you risk by embracing that kind of attitude about yourself? What do you stand to gain?

4. We've talked about the idea of *feeding* anger—that some people, situations, and circumstances can cause anger to build up inside of us. But what about feeding humility? What are some ways that you can feed humility to cause it to grow in your heart and mind?

5. Read the excerpt below from chapter 24 of *Unoffendable*, and then answer the questions that follow.

> So let's review: Choosing to be unoffendable means choosing to be humble. Not only that, the practice *teaches* humility. Once you've decided you can't control other people; once you've reconciled yourself to the fact that the world, and its people, are broken; once you've realized your own moral failure before God; once you've abandoned the idea that your significance comes from anything other than God, you're growing in humility, and that's exactly where God wants us all.
>
> It's contrary to seemingly everything in our culture, but the more we divest ourselves of ourselves, the better our lives get. Jesus told us as much. He said if we'd give up our lives, for his sake, we'd find real life.
>
> When we surrender our perceived "rights," when we let go of our attempts to manipulate, we find—surprise!—joy.

I've seen it happen in my own life, in little bits. I'm still learning. But I'm so glad someone told me to choose to be unoffendable, because something clicked in my understanding of what it means to follow Jesus. It turns out that life is not only more joy-filled for me but more attractive to others.

I have to die to myself. What I'm finding is it doesn't happen all at once, and it's simultaneously simple to understand and arduous to actually do. But little by little, I think I'm seeing what God is up to.[16]

Think about that word *joy*. Use the space below to express what joy means in your life. Draw a picture, make a list, tell a story . . . whatever you prefer.

The seemingly crazy promise of Jesus is that by dying to ourselves, we will experience true, authentic, abundant life. When have you experienced that reality?

6. When trying to learn a new skill, it's often helpful to set short-term and long-term goals. Use the space below to do that regarding this idea of becoming unoffendable. What steps or landmarks will help you reach that ultimate goal?

What are your goals for becoming unoffendable in the next two weeks?

What are your goals for the next year?

What are your goals for the next five years?

Day 2

FREEDOM AND BLESSINGS

What benefits do you receive by choosing to become unoffendable? For one thing, you gain *freedom*. You don't have to give harmful people room in your mind or your heart for the rest of your life. You can let them go along with the anger they produced. You don't have to continue to be weighed down by bitterness or rage or the desire for revenge.

You can be free. You can focus on the parts of your life that build you up and bring about blessings. The apostle Paul addressed this kind of freedom several times in his epistle to the Galatians. In the passage below, you will notice that his instructions on living freely culminate in the wonderful blessing we call the "fruit of the Spirit." Read this passage through several times, and then answer the questions that follow.

> [13] You, my brothers and sisters, were called to be free. But do not use your freedom to indulge the flesh; rather, serve one another humbly in love. [14] For the entire law is fulfilled in keeping this one command: "Love your neighbor as yourself." [15] If you bite and devour each other, watch out or you will be destroyed by each other.
>
> [16] So I say, walk by the Spirit, and you will not gratify the desires of the flesh. [17] For the flesh desires what is contrary to the Spirit, and the Spirit what is contrary to the flesh. They are in conflict with each other, so that you are not to do whatever you want. [18] But if you are led by the Spirit, you are not under the law.
>
> [19] The acts of the flesh are obvious: sexual immorality, impurity and debauchery; [20] idolatry and witchcraft; hatred, discord, jealousy, fits of rage, selfish ambition, dissensions, factions [21] and envy; drunkenness, orgies, and the like. I warn you, as I did before, that those who live like this will not inherit the kingdom of God.
>
> [22] But the fruit of the Spirit is love, joy, peace, forbearance, kindness, goodness, faithfulness, [23] gentleness and self-control. Against such things there is no law.
>
> Galatians 5:13–23

1. What catches your attention in Paul's words in this passage? Why?

2. Circle any words or phrases in the passage above that connect with the theme of anger. How do those words or phrases support the themes we have been exploring in this study?

3. Paul reminded followers of Jesus about their Lord's command to "love your neighbor as yourself." Who in your life has been a model of loving others that way? What has that person done that stands out to you?

4. Look at the "acts of the flesh" that Paul lists in verses 19–21. Which of those descriptions have you struggled with in the past? In the present?

5. Now look at the "fruit of the Spirit" that Paul lists in verses 22–23. Where do you see a connection between that fruit and choosing to live in a way that is unoffendable?

6. Choosing humility and forgiveness will produce freedom—that's the promise we have been exploring in these pages. Look again at the "acts of the flesh." What are two steps you can take this week to intentionally move away from those acts and move toward freedom?

Action step 1:

Action step 2:

Day 3

BACK TO THE BEGINNING

Ready to go back where we started?

In the first session, we explored the crazy idea that Christians should not hold onto anger—even "righteous" anger. Instead, we should recognize anger as something that is corrosive and destructive and get rid of it as quickly as possible.

Now, as we discussed, such a suggestion inevitably leads people to ask about the verse in the Bible that says, "In your anger do not sin." This verse has been a primary reason why so many Christians believe anger is not only acceptable on some occasions but also required.

Now that we've been studying this topic for six sessions, let's go back to that verse, along with its surrounding context, and see what it really says. Read the following passage out loud, and then answer the questions that follow.

> [25] Therefore each of you must put off falsehood and speak truthfully to your neighbor, for we are all members of one body. [26] "In your anger do not sin": Do not let the sun go down while you are still angry, [27] and do not give the devil a foothold. [28] Anyone who has been stealing must steal no longer, but must work, doing something useful with their own hands, that they may have something to share with those in need.
>
> [29] Do not let any unwholesome talk come out of your mouths, but only what is helpful for building others up according to their needs, that it may benefit those who listen. [30] And do not grieve the Holy Spirit of God, with whom you were sealed for the day of redemption. [31] Get rid of all bitterness, rage and anger, brawling and slander, along with every form of malice. [32] Be kind and compassionate to one another, forgiving each other, just as in Christ God forgave you.
>
> Ephesians 4:25–32

1. Circle each of the commands included in the verses above. Overall, how would you summarize Paul's instructions about anger?

2. "Don't let the sun go down on your wrath" is a common saying in the world today, though we typically use it in terms of relationships—we should resolve all conflicts before the end of the day. But is it necessary for you to resolve the source of your anger *before* you let go of that anger? Explain your answer.

3. Now that you've almost completed this study, use the scale below to evaluate your ability to recognize and release your anger.

On a scale of 1 (slowly) to 10 (quickly), how quickly are you able to identify feelings of anger in your mind and heart?

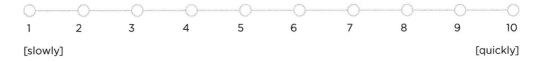

1   2   3   4   5   6   7   8   9   10

[slowly]   [quickly]

On a scale of 1 (easy) to 10 (difficult), how hard is it for you to let go of anger when you experience it?

1   2   3   4   5   6   7   8   9   10

[easy]   [difficult]

On a scale of 1 (a little) to 10 (a lot), how much have you improved in your ability to handle anger over the course of this study?

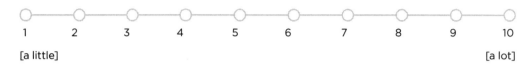

1	2	3	4	5	6	7	8	9	10

[a little]   [a lot]

4. Imagine you had a friend who was dealing with an anger issue. Your friend not only experiences a lot of anger, but he or she also carries it around inside. How would you explain the process of releasing anger to that friend?

5. Look again at Paul's words in verse 31. Where do you see the church as a whole struggling to follow this command?

6. Now look at verse 32. Where do Christians in today's world have opportunities to demonstrate forgiveness and compassion? Where do you, specifically, have those opportunities right now?

Day 4

CELEBRATE!

Studies like this can trend toward the serious . . . even somber. You've just spent several weeks thinking about concepts such as anger, bitterness, wrath, and unforgiveness. Mind you, there are good reasons to explore those themes, and hopefully the time you have invested has been worthwhile. But there's been a lot of emotional investment on your part.

Now, as we conclude this study, it's time to celebrate. Begin by connecting with a member from the group one last time and working through the questions and suggestions below. As you do this, it should serve as a positive finale for this resource.

1. Start the discussion by talking about your favorite moments from the study—both in the group sections and personal study sections. What have you enjoyed the most?

2. What are some of the ways your life has been impacted in a positive way as you have become more aware of what it means to be unoffendable?

3. Now focus on your partner. What have you appreciated most about their presence and support in recent weeks as you've gone through this study?

4. Use the space below to draw a picture of yourself a year from now. Specifically, draw yourself being *unoffendable*. Create a scene, symbol, or something else that represents what you will be like as you continue to grow in letting go of your anger and extending forgiveness to others. When you've finished, explain the drawing to your partner.

5. What emotions are you experiencing most strongly as you come to the end of this study?

6. Finish by spending a few moments in prayer with your partner. Praise God for the work that he has done in your lives and praise him for the opportunity he has given you to live an unoffendable life. Pray for your partner and then verbally commit to embracing radical forgiveness in obedience to God's Word and God's will. Use the space below to record any last reflections or takeaways that you want to keep with you after this study is concluded.

Day 5

WRAP IT UP

Use this time to go back and complete any of the study and reflection questions from previous days this week that you weren't able to finish. Make note of any revelations you've had and reflect on any growth or personal insights you've gained. Finally, discuss with your group what studies you might want to go through next and when you will next meet together.

LEADER'S GUIDE

Thank you for your willingness to lead your group through this study! What you have chosen to do is valuable and will make a great difference in the lives of others. The rewards of being a leader are different from those of participating, and we hope that as you lead you will find your own journey with the God of the How and When deepened by this experience.

Unoffendable is a six-session Bible study built around video content and small-group interaction. As the group leader, imagine yourself as the host of a party. Your job is to take care of your guests by managing the details so that when your guests arrive, they can focus on one another and on the interaction around the topic for that session.

Your role as the group leader is not to answer all the questions or reteach the content—the video, book, and study guide will do most of that work. Your job is to guide the experience and cultivate your small group into a connected and engaged community. This will make it a place for members to process, question, and reflect—not necessarily receive more instruction.

There are several elements in this leader's guide that will help you as you structure your study and reflection time, so be sure to follow along and take advantage of each one.

Before You Begin

Before your first meeting, make sure the group members have a copy of this study guide. Alternately, you can hand out the study guides at your first meeting and give the members some time to look over the material and ask any preliminary questions. Also make sure they are aware that they have access to the streaming videos at any time by following the instructions printed on the inside front cover. During your first meeting, ask the members to provide their name, phone number, and email address so you can keep in touch with them.

Generally, the ideal size for a group is eight to ten people, which will ensure that everyone has enough time to participate in discussions. If you have more people, you might want to break up the main group into smaller subgroups. Encourage those who show up at the first meeting to commit to attending the duration of the study, as this will help the group members get to know one another, create stability for the group, and help you know how to best prepare to lead them through the material.

Each of the sessions begins with an opening reflection in the "Welcome" section. The questions that follow in the "Connect" section serve as an icebreaker to get the group members thinking about the topic. Some people may want to tell a long story in response to one of these questions, but the goal is to keep the answers brief. Ideally, you want everyone in the group to get a chance to answer, so try to keep the responses to a minute or less. If you have talkative group members, say up front that everyone needs to limit their answer to one minute.

Give the group members a chance to answer, but also tell them to feel free to pass if they wish. With the rest of the study, it's generally not a good idea to have everyone answer every question—a free-flowing discussion is more desirable. But with the opening icebreaker questions, you can go around the circle. Encourage shy people to share, but don't force them.

At your first meeting, let the group members know each session contains a personal study section they can use to continue to engage with the content until the next meeting. While this is optional, it will help them cement the concepts presented during the group study time. Let them know that if they choose to do so, they can watch the video for the next session by accessing the streaming code found on the inside front cover of their studies. Invite them to bring any questions and insights to your next meeting, especially if they had a breakthrough moment or didn't understand something.

Preparation for Each Session

As the leader, there are a few things you should do to prepare for each meeting:

- Read through the session. This will help you become more familiar with the content and know how to structure the discussion times.

- Decide how the videos will be used. Determine whether you want the members to watch the videos ahead of time (again, via the streaming access code found on the inside front cover) or together as a group.

- Decide which questions you want to discuss. Based on the length of your group discussions, you may not be able to get through all the questions. So look over the recommendations for the suggested and additional questions in each session and choose which ones you definitely want to cover.

- Be familiar with the questions you want to discuss. When the group meets, you'll be watching the clock, so make sure you are familiar with the questions that you have selected. In this way, you will ensure that you have the material more deeply in your mind than your group members.

- Pray for your group. Pray for your group members and ask God to lead them as they study his Word.

In many cases, there will be no one "right" answer to the question. Answers will vary, especially when the group members are being asked to share their personal experiences.

Structuring the Discussion Time

You will need to determine with your group how long you want to meet so you can plan your time accordingly. Suggested times for each section have been provided in this study guide, and if you adhere to these times, your group will meet for ninety minutes, as noted below. If you want to meet for two hours, follow the times given in the right-hand column:

Section	90 Minutes	120 Minutes
CONNECT (discuss one or more of the opening questions for the session)	15 minutes	20 minutes
WATCH (watch the teaching material together and take notes)	20 minutes	20 minutes
DISCUSS (discuss the study questions you selected ahead of time)	35 minutes	50 minutes
RESPOND (write down key takeaways)	10 minutes	15 minutes
PRAY (pray together and dismiss)	10 minutes	15 minutes

As the group leader, it is up to you to keep track of the time and keep things on schedule. You might want to set a timer for each segment so both you and the group members know when your time is up. (There are some good phone apps for timers that play a gentle chime or other pleasant sound instead of a disruptive noise.)

Don't be concerned if the group members are quiet or slow to share. People are often quiet when they are pulling together their ideas, and this might be a new experience for them. Just ask a question and let it hang in the air until someone shares. You can then say, "Thank you. What about others? What came to you when you watched that portion of the teaching?"

Group Dynamics

Leading a group through the *Unoffendable Bible Study* will prove to be a highly rewarding experience both for you and for your group members. But you still may encounter challenges along the way! Discussions can get off track. Group members may not be sensitive to the needs and ideas of others. Some might worry they will be expected to talk about matters that make them feel awkward. Others may express comments that result in disagreements. To help ease this strain on you and the group, consider the following ground rules:

- When someone raises a question or comment that is off the main topic, suggest that you deal with it another time, or, if you feel led to go in that direction, let the group know you will be spending some time discussing it.

- If someone asks a question that you don't know how to answer, admit it and move on. At your discretion, feel free to invite group members to comment on questions that call for personal experience.

- If you find one or two people are dominating the discussion time, direct a few questions to others in the group. Outside the main group time, ask the more dominating members to help you draw out the quieter ones. Work to make them a part of the solution instead of part of the problem.

- When a disagreement occurs, encourage the group members to process the matter in love. Encourage those on opposite sides to restate what they heard the other side say about the matter, and then invite each side to evaluate if that perception is accurate. Lead the group in examining other Scriptures related to the topic and look for common ground.

When any of these issues arise, encourage your group members to follow these words from Scripture: "Love one another" (John 13:34), "If it is possible, as far as it depends on you, live at peace with everyone" (Romans 12:18), "Whatever is true . . . noble . . . right . . . if anything is excellent or praiseworthy—think about such things" (Philippians 4:8), and, "Be quick to listen, slow to speak and slow to become angry" (James 1:19). This will make your group time more rewarding and beneficial for everyone who attends.

Thank you again for leading your group. You are making a difference in your group members' lives and having an impact on their journey toward becoming unoffendable.

ENDNOTES

1. Raymond Novaco, professor of psychology at the University of California at Irvine, quoted in Elizabeth Chang, "Americans Are Living in a Big 'Anger Incubator,'" The Washington Post, June 30, 2020, https://www.washingtonpost.com/lifestyle/wellness/anger-control-protests-masks-coronavirus/2020/06/29/a1e882d0-b279-11ea-8758-bfd1d045525a_story.html).

2. *The Cambridge Dictionary*, s.v. "offended," https://dictionary.cambridge.org/us/dictionary/english/offended.

3. Brant Hansen, *Unoffendable* (Nashville, TN: W Publishing, 2022), p. 12.

4. Hansen, *Unoffendable*, p. 20.

5. Hansen, *Unoffendable*, p. 35.

6. Dictionary.com, s.v. "self-righteousness," https://www.dictionary.com/browse/self-righteous.

7. Hansen, *Unoffendable*, p. 50.

8. Hansen, *Unoffendable*, p. 82.

9. Hansen, *Unoffendable*, pp. 63–64.

10. Hansen, *Unoffendable*, pp. 91–92.

11. Hansen, *Unoffendable*, pp. 121–122.

12. Rachel Denhollander, cited in Morgan Lee, "My Larry Nassar Testimony Went Viral, but There's More to the Gospel Than Forgiveness," *Christianity Today,* January 31, 2018, https://www.christianitytoday.com/ct/2018/january-web-only/rachael-denhollander-larry-nassar-forgiveness-gospel.html.

13. Hansen, *Unoffendable*, p. 127.

14. Hansen, *Unoffendable*, p. 143.

15. Hansen, *Unoffendable*, p. 181.

16. Hansen, *Unoffendable*, p. 188.

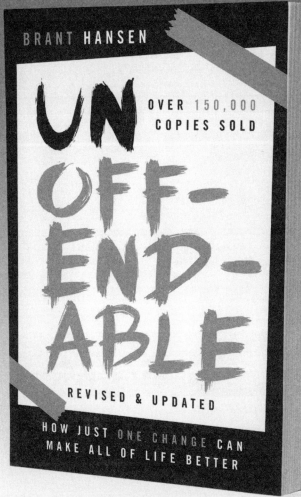

 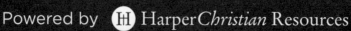

From the Publisher

GREAT STUDIES

ARE EVEN BETTER WHEN THEY'RE SHARED!

Help others find this study:

- Post a review at your favorite online bookseller.

- Post a picture on a social media account and share why you enjoyed it.

- Send a note to a friend who would also love it—or, better yet, go through it with them!

Thanks for helping others grow their faith!